The geography of public welfare provision

Regional variations in public welfare provision are the cause of some of the most heated debates about the public service sector. Very often the geographical factors inherent in these anomalies are ignored. *The Geography of Public Welfare Provision* shows just how important these factors are, and introduces the reader to a crucial aspect of Britain's welfare service system.

Comparing the variable patterns of welfare we observe in the population with the service provision made by local authorities and other agencies, Sarah Curtis considers how far these are fair and equitable. She examines the socio-geographical characteristics of groups of people who are most vulnerable in society, and most likey to need to use services, focusing especially on three groups: the elderly, the young and ethnic minorities. Exploring the recent restructuring of the welfare system, the book charts how this has affected the relationship between public, private and voluntary sectors of welfare service provision.

With up-to-date information drawn from extensive research, *The Geography of Public Welfare Provision* provides a detailed account of the British welfare system relevant to students and local authority policy makers in Britain and many other countries.

Sarah Curtis has taught in the Geography Department at Queen Mary College, London, since 1981.

The geography of public welfare provision

Sarah Curtis

R
ROUTLEDGE
London and New York

First published 1989 by Routledge
11 New Fetter Lane, London EC4P 4EE
29 West 35th Street, New York, NY 10001

© 1989 Sarah Curtis

Typeset by LaserScript Limited, Mitcham, Surrey
Printed and bound in Great Britain by
Biddles Ltd, Guildford and King's Lynn

British Library Cataloguing in Publication Data
Curtis, Sarah, *1954–*
    The geography of public welfare provision.
    1. Great Britain. Welfare services.
    Geographical aspects
    I. Title
    361'.941

ISBN 0–415–03472–8

Library of Congress Cataloging in Publication Data
Curtis, Sarah, 1954–
    The geography of public welfare provision / Sarah Curtis.
    p. cm. — (Geography, environment, and planning)
    Bibliography: p.
    ISBN 0–415–03472–8
    1. Public welfare—Great Britain—Regional disparities.
    I. Title. II. Series.
    HV245.C87 1989
    361'.941–dc19   88–28714
                                                                  CIP

Contents

Contents

List of figures and tables

Figures

Tables

Figures and tables

Acknowledgements

I should like to thank all those who have helped and advised with the production of this book, especially Brian Blundell (London Borough of Greenwich), Professor David Smith (Queen Mary College), Professor Neil Wrigley (UWIST), and my parents, Leonard and Diana Curtis. All their help and support was much appreciated, although of course I take sole responsibility for the contents of this book.

Chapter one

Welfare objectives and socio-spatial inequality

Introduction: the geography of public welfare provision

This book examines the geographical dimensions of public provision for the welfare of members of society. The focus is on personal services, supplied to individual consumers to promote their individual welfare, by agencies which are organized and financed, at least in part, as a state-operated system. These services are referred to as 'public welfare provision' in this text. Geographical factors do not always receive due attention in the debate over fairness and value for money in the public service sector. This book attempts to redress the balance by emphasizing geographical issues in the debate. The objective is therefore to describe the geographical dimensions of welfare provision, and to consider some of their implications for equity and efficiency in the public sector.

The concept of welfare used in this book is essentially individualistic, and can be expressed as the well-being, or 'real income', in terms of material and spiritual resources, enjoyed by individuals and groups of people in a society. One objective of this book is to compare the variable patterns of welfare we observe in a society with the welfare provision made by the public sector, and to consider whether these are fair and equitable. Much of the discussion is therefore concerned with the socio-geographical characteristics of people who are likely to need to use services, and with spatial patterns in welfare service provision.

The discussion here is particularly concerned with the role of local government authorities, as an important public sector agency providing personal welfare services, and with the interface between local government and other public, private, and voluntary agencies providing complementary or supplementary or alternative services. Health care has been thoroughly studied by medical geographers for some time, but despite certain notable exceptions (e.g. Bennett 1980, 1982; Pinch 1985), the geographical perspective on local authority

1

activity has not received such comprehensive attention. This text is intended to complement other work on the geography of services by providing an overview of the role of the local authority in providing personal welfare services. It has been written at a time when local government agencies are undergoing rapid change in their functions with respect to welfare services. This, then, is a particularly interesting time to examine the geographical aspects of these changes. The evolution of the welfare provision functions of local government and of links with their partners in the other sectors are discussed in Chapters 2 and 3.

For public services, the interpretation of need is also important to the analysis of provision. The spatial distribution of welfare provision bears some relation to the geography of need, but the correspondence is not a perfect one. Need should therefore be assessed from the perspective of population characteristics rather than being based on current patterns of service activity. Ideas and approaches from social geography should make a significant contribution to the identification and assessment of need. The later chapters of this book consider, from a socio-geographical perspective, the needs of some particularly vulnerable groups in the population, and review methods to assess relative needs of populations in different geographical areas.

The discussion focuses on the British case, and especially England, to examine the provision of welfare by local authorities and by other agencies of the public, private, and informal sector. However, the relationships and processes observed here and many of the general conclusions are not entirely confined to the UK. In other European countries, and in the USA, the same issues are being debated, and lessons from the British experience have a wider relevance. This chapter introduces some ideas about the nature of welfare services, and presents some evidence of the social and spatial inequalities which are relevant to welfare provision.

Public goods: geographical factors and impurity

The idea of a public good, taken from welfare economics, provides a useful starting-point for a study of welfare services. Samuelson (1954) and Musgrave and Musgrave (1980: ch. 3) have described how pure public goods differ from private goods because they are provided collectively, and supplied jointly to the population, so that no one is excluded from consuming the good, and nobody can reject it or opt out of consuming it. A typical example might be fluoridation of the water supply.

In fact few public goods and services are 'pure', in that they are consumed and benefited from jointly and equally by the population, and to the extent that they are non-joint, they may be considered 'impure' public goods. Bennett (1980) considers how the the degree of jointness may vary for spatial and non-spatial reasons. Some directly spatial factors are associated with non-jointness; tapering, jurisdictional partitioning, and externality effects, which are explained below. Jointness also varies according to the extent that members of the public differ in their need, eligibility, and demands for public goods. As we shall see in later chapters, demographic, economic, and social factors affecting need and demand for care also show clear geographical patterning.

Smith (1977) has described how, for services provided from a facility at a particular location, spatial tapering of a public good results from variation in the utility of the service for consumers with proximity to the source of provision (Figure 1.1). Usually the benefits decline with distance from the source, as accessibility costs increase to the limit of the range of the good or service, where costs of obtaining the good outweigh the benefits. However, proximity to facilities may have positive or negative benefits for the population of an area. Some facilities (e.g. nuclear power stations, fire stations) have disbenefits associated with close proximity, for instance due to their nuisance or

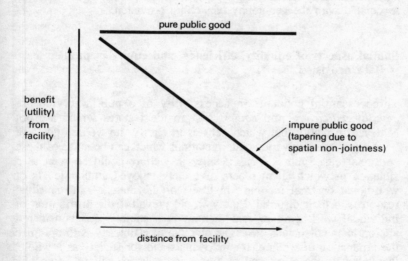

Figure 1.1 The effects of tapering on public goods and services

polluting effects, so that in some cases distance decay in utility from the source of supply is not straightfoward. Geographical factors of position and location contribute to the 'impurity' of public goods. The location of facilities in relation to the population they serve affects the utility derived from public services, and contributes to the non-jointness of public welfare provision.

Jursidictional partitioning also produces spatial non-jointness. The geographical division of populations for the purposes of provision of public welfare means that local divisions of service administrations have responsiblity to provide statutory welfare services to populations with very different need profiles. Eligibility rules and levels of service provision may vary from one jurisdiction to another, so that people in similar circumstances may receive different treatment according to their area of residence. This book considers the partitioning of the UK space between local authorities, and their varying activities as public welfare providers, and the resulting non-jointness in the availability of public services for the population.

Although services may be provided for the population in particular areas, there may be some spilling over of the costs and benefits from one area to another. For example, a public park provided by one authority may be enjoyed by people living outside that authority. These externality effects further complicate the pattern of accessibility associated with the geography of welfare provision.

Spatial aspects of equality, efficiency, and equity in public welfare provision

Three essential concepts in accessibility of a public service are *equality, efficiency,* and *equity*. All are ideal states which are not achieved in reality, but which help us to clarify the welfare goals of a society. There are various interpretations which can be made of these concepts (e.g. Smith 1977). Equality in welfare could be seen as a situation in which all members of society enjoyed similar levels of well-being or 'real income', in terms of the material and spiritual resources at their disposal. Equity would prevail if the distribution of individual well-being or real income in a society was considered appropriate and socially just. The pinciple of efficiency is to optimize the production of welfare, for individuals and for society as a whole, in relation to the effort and resources invested in welfare by society collectively and by its members individually.

An important theme in this book is that of inequality in welfare and in access to services for different population groups. The evidence for inequality in welfare is discussed later in this chapter, with particular reference to income, health, and social circumstances; education; housing; and mobility.

There are various ways in which inequality can be summarized using statistical techniques to analyse social indicators: commonly used measures are the Gini coefficient and the Lorenz curve. These have been developed by Le Grand and colleagues to compare individuals (e.g. Le Grand and Illsley 1987), but they may also be used to compare the population of geographical areas (Smith 1977: 134–5).

The geographical scale of analysis may be crucial to studies of inequality. Broad equality between large regions may, for example, disguise considerable herogeneity between smaller areas within regions. An apparently well-endowed area may contain smaller pockets of deprivation. Later in this book the question of scale is also seen to be significant to the organization of welfare services in the debate over local vs. regional or central government responsibility for welfare.

Geographical scale is an important consideration for the efficiency of public services. The inequalities of public welfare provision, which form the principal subject of this book, exist partly because of the exigencies of efficiency of resource use. Geographical criteria of efficiency include optimum catchment area and population size. We can envisage a hierarchy of public goods according to the scale of area over which services can be efficiently provided. Regional public goods are those for which economies of scale make it most appropriate to provide for large geographical areas at a single facility. These are often specialist services which are required only for a small proportion of the population, or services whose consumers are highly mobile. Local goods are better provided for the population of a small geographical area. This may be because the service is needed by a large proportion of the population, because it is not possible to make provision satisfactorily for large numbers of people in one place or because the distance decay effects are very strong for people using the service (Figure 1.2).

For example, it could be argued that polytechnics as institutions of higher education operate most efficiently at the regional scale since they need to be large to support the range of specialist courses required, and students can be drawn from a wide geographical area, without significantly detracting from the utility and accessibility of the service. At the other end of the scale, an example of a local public service might be a state primary school, which is required by most of the young people in the neighbourhood. Young children and their mothers are a group for whom the friction of distance is relatively high (for reasons discussed in Chapter 4), and the provision of a

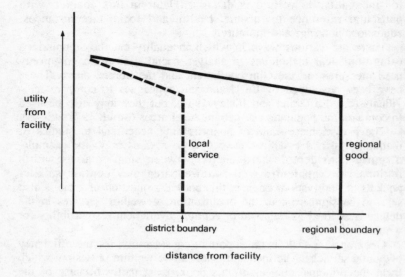

Figure 1.2 Local and regional public services

good-quality education is problematic in very large and anonymous institutions.

Some services need to be provided on a domiciliary basis (for example, home help for mothers with young children, or for elderly people). For such domiciliary services, the tapering effect associated with distance from the location of a facility will probably have little importance for the utility of the service for the consumer. However, wide dispersal of consumers in a sparsely populated rural area may affect the cost of the operation to providers of domiciliary care. Varying policies between service catchment areas can significantly affect the pattern of domiciliary provision and the availability of the service for consumers.

Thus the concepts of the service area and range of a good may be relevant to determining suitable administrative systems for services. Writers such as Abler, Adams, and Gould (1971), Massam (1975), and Thisse and Zoller (1983) have discussed the question of optimization of the location–allocation problem for public welfare provision, and a number of computer algorithms have been developed to analyse the implications of the positioning of facilities and districting for public services (Wilson 1974; Clarke and Wilson 1987; Mayhew and Leonardi 1982; Mayhew 1986).

The solutions to algorithms for the location–allocation problem in public welfare provision depend on the type of distribution which is desired, and will always lead us back ultimately to fundamental questions of need for services and equity. In this book it is argued that need should be defined with regard to the view from the community rather than based on the current pattern of welfare provision. Approaches to the assessment of relative needs of different populations are considered in Chapter 7.

Assessment of equity depends on the view of a just distribution of public goods. Examples of criteria for judging distributions include the utilitarian view (maximizing the overall benefit), pareto optimality (which accepts distributions improving the overall utility without worsening the position of the least privileged consumers), and constrained inequality (which limits the range of variation in access to public welfare services) (Smith 1977). Equity in access to services may not therefore be equivalent to perfect equality. The choice of a suitable model for public welfare provision is ultimately determined by considerations of political ideology and philosophical theories of need and social justice. Some alternative definitions of what comprises social justice in welfare provision are considered in more detail in Chapter 8. Ideas of social justice have a geographical dimension, as shown in Harvey's well-known exposition of the problem of social justice in the city (Harvey 1973). Davies (1968) introduced the idea of *territorial justice*, defined as a situation in which the distribution of society's goods between areas corresponds to the varying needs of those areas. Territorial justice is a fundamental and recurring theme in this book.

Assessing social inequalities

Any modern society comprises a variety of different social groups whose position in terms of power, resources, and privilege differs. Social class is a commonly used concept to categorize these groups. A class can be described sociologically as a group sharing similar values, position in society, and the sense of a common identity. The idea of class also carries connotations in political theory. Pinch (1985) summarizes the Weberian view of social classes as groups with differential access to society's scarce resources, that is on the basis of patterns of consumption, and contrasts this interpretation with the Marxist view of class as a division between the working class who are wage-earners and the proprietorial class who control capital – i.e. a distinction based on differences in the role of the two groups in the production process.

Often therefore the idea of class is operationalized in terms of position in the economic structure. In the UK occupational group is the most commonly used indicator, as defined in the Registrar-General's Classification (OPCS 1980a). The classification distinguishes seventeen socio-economic groups, which are summarized in terms of 'social position' into six social classes, ranging from the professional and managerial classes I and II, through junior non-manual group III, to skilled manual workers (group IIIm) to semi- and unskilled workers in classes IV and V.

The geographical distribution of occupational social classes in the UK space is variable, with a large proportion of those in the less privileged manual groups in the north and west of the country, while the professional and non-manual groups are especially concentrated in the south and east (see Table 1.1). This distribution is in part the historical legacy of the mining, processing, and manufacturing industries which grew up in the Industrial Revolution in the eighteenth and nineteenth centuries, and in part to the concentration of commercial and tertiary activity in the south-east today.

Occupational social class is a useful way of summarizing social position, and it continues to be an important aspect of social differentiation (Marshall *et al.* 1988). However, it is today rather inadequate as an expression of some socio-economic divisions in society. The occupational class of families is generally based on the occupational group of the person identified as the (normally male) 'head of household'. However, for women, especially spouses, and for the retired or economically inactive members of the population, such as children, students, etc., the classification may be inappropriate. Evans (1983) takes issue with the assumption that a woman's socio-economic status will be primarily deterimined by her husband or father. Not all women have access to resources and rewards of the occupation of their menfolk (Pahl 1980, 1985). There are also many households which are not wholly reliant on the income from a male wage-earner. The social and economic position of retired people is not always reliably indicated by their last paid occupation. In short, factors such as age, gender, and ethnicity are also important dimensions of social position and are associated with both position in the production process and consumption patterns of the 'goods' produced by our society. These are given consideration in Chapters 4–6, where we consider some of the particularly vulnerable groups in society and their needs for public welfare.

There is known to be inequality in welfare between social groups in many countries. In the UK this has been the subject of study and debate for a long time, and the comprehensive body of evidence describing these inqualities makes the British case a particularly interesting one to consider. The following sections review some of this

Table 1.1 Social class distribution by standard regions of the UK: 1981

Standard region	Percentage in social class					
	I Professionals	II Managers	IIINM Junior non-manual	IIIM Skilled manual	IV Semi-skilled manual	V Unskilled manual
Northern	3.5	14.6	7.6	29.8	13.0	5.3
North-western	4.1	16.8	8.7	26.7	13.5	5.0
Yorkshire and Humberside	3.3	16.9	8.0	28.8	13.2	4.4
West Midlands	3.8	17.4	7.8	29.4	14.2	3.9
East Midlands	3.8	18.1	8.1	29.9	13.2	3.6
South-east	5.8	22.2	11.1	23.0	10.5	3.5
East Anglia	4.4	19.6	8.3	25.6	12.5	3.5
South-west	4.7	19.9	9.2	23.8	10.9	3.1
England	4.6	19.2	9.3	26.1	12.1	3.9
Wales	3.7	16.6	7.5	26.6	11.8	4.5
Scotland	4.2	16.4	8.4	27.3	13.2	5.0
Northern Ireland	3.2	18.6	7.7	23.6	10.6	4.8
United Kingdom	4.5	18.8	9.1	26.1	12.2	4.1

Source: Central Statistical Office, *Regional Trends*, 1982.
Note: Percentages do not add up to 100%; the remaining population was inactive or employed in the armed forces.

evidence, and particularly the geographical manifestations of the inequalities.

Inequality of income

Income differences have been argued to be the most fundamental aspect of inequality (Le Grand 1982). Since the nineteenth century studies have shown a significant proportion of the population in poverty. For example, Charles Booth's surveys of the life and labour of the people of London (Simey and Simey 1960) showed the distribution of different classes of family, distinguishing between those viewed as the deserving poor, with inadequate incomes, and those families who were seen to be suffering hardship as a result of dissipation. A moral distinction was therefore made, reflecting the judgemental element involved in any definition of poverty. Using information supplied by the school board inspectors, Booth was able to plot house by house the spatial distribution of these families. His coloured maps are a fascinating historical record, showing the poorer households in black and purple in the alleys and mews of the East End of London, contrasting with the wealthy gentry, shown in red, in the larger homes facing the main streets.

Rowntree made his first study of York in 1899, first published in 1901 as *A Study of Town Life*, and defined a poverty line. According to the survey results, 10 per cent of the population was in 'primary poverty' (lacking the means to obtain the minimum necessities for the maintenance of merely physical efficiency), and a futher 18 per cent were in 'secondary poverty' (income would support basic physical efficiency if it were not for other expenditure either useful or wasteful) (Briggs 1961). Subsequent studies of a cohort from York in the 1950s also revealed about one-third of the population living in poverty. These surveys were followed up more recently, by Atkinson, Maynard, and Trinder (1983), demonstrating that income inequalities persist from one generation to the next.

Differences in absolute and relative income levels are still an important aspect of inequality in Britain at the present day. The Royal Commission on the Distribution of Income and Wealth (GB. Parliament 1979a) has examined trends in inequalities. During the period 1949–76 these seemed to be reducing, as income shares became more even among the British population. However, in the years since 1979 this trend has reversed and inequality seems to be increasing, as shown in Table 1.2, which indicates the variation in the proportion of total income accruing to the wealthiest 10 per cent of the population.

At the national scale, sample surveys such as the *Family Expenditure Survey* (OPCS 1987) and the *General Household Survey*

Table 1.2 Changing inequality of income shares in the UK: 1949–82 (percentages)

Rank of income group	Share of total after tax income			
	*1949**	*1976–7**	*1978–9†*	*1981–2†*
Top 100%	27.1	22.4	23.4	25.6
Next 40%	46.4	40.6	50.4	49.2
Bottom 50%	26.5	37.0	26.2	25.2

* Royal Commission on Distribution of Income and Wealth, *Report 7: Wealth, Income and Equality*, 1979.
† *New Society*, 16 August 1984.

(OPCS 1986a) show differences in income and family expenditure patterns between different social groups and populations of different regions. Table 1.3 shows the average expenditure of families according to occupational group. Recent figures for the average income of the populations of different regions of the UK shows that average weekly normal disposable income varied from £218 in the south-east to £155 in the north in 1985/6 (see Figure 1.3).

Low income is a fundamental dimension of inequality because it is related to other aspects of 'well-being' – such as education, health, and housing – which are of special interest in this book. Poverty is significant not so much because of absolute levels of income, but rather in terms of the expectations of the society in which poverty is found. Townsend's (1979) survey of poverty in the UK shows us that relative poverty relates not only to subsistence income, but to various aspects of lifestyle. The person who cannot afford a winter coat, a Sunday roast meal, or an annual holiday may be relatively deprived compared with the average expectation of today's society. These norms vary over time, and between different societies, so that the idea of deprivation is essentially value laden. In Chapters 7 and 8 we return to the problem of defining deprivation and how it relates to need for welfare provision.

Inequalities in education

Access to education is related to other aspects of life chances, especially employment prospects. The theory of the cycle of

11

Table 1.3   Average weekly expenditure of households in Britain, by occupational group of the head of household: 1986

	Average weekly expenditure	
	Total (£)	Per person (£)
Professional and technical	300.96	105
Administrative and managerial	287.92	97
Teacher	278.66	95
Clerical	192.03	80
Skilled manual	209.12	66
Semi-skilled manual	177.55	62
Unskilled manual	159.43	60
All with employed head of household	229.64	79

Source: OPCS, 1986a.

disadvantage (Wedge and Prosser 1973) stresses childhood experience of educational deprivation as an important element in future deprivation. Consumption of non-compulsory education (nursery schooling and further education) differs between social classes, and between areas, and this is discussed in Chapter 4. Education is now compulsory for all children up to the age of 16 years, but the outcome varies; Halsey, Heath, and Ridge (1980) showed that among the professional classes, in England and Wales, more than half of children obtained Ordinary- or Advanced-level qualifications, more than a quarter obtained A-levels, and 20 per cent went to university. In contrast, among working-class children 12 per cent obtained O-level qualifications, 7 per cent A-levels, and only 5 per cent went to university. The figures in Table 1.4 also show the regional variation in attainment at school-leaving age in 1978–9. The proportion going on to full-time education was higher in non-metropolitan areas, especially in the south-east and the Midlands in 1978–9, while the proportion leaving school without qualifications was higher in the metropolitan areas, especially in London.

It seems that these geographical disparities partly reflect variations in social factors. Gray and Jesson (1987) have standardized the rate of school achievement (measured as the percentage of children

Average normal weekly
disposable income in
1985 and 1986.

Average for UK = £184

SCOTLAND
£170

NORTHERN
IRELAND
£159

NORTH
£155

YORKSHIRE &
HUMBERSIDE
£159

NORTH
WEST
£168

EAST
MIDLANDS
£178

£171
WEST
MIDLANDS

EAST
ANGLIA
£168

£168
WALES

SOUTH EAST
£218

GREATER LONDON
215

SOUTH WEST
£192

Figure 1.3 Average normal weekly disposable income: 1985 and 1986

13

Table 1.4   Educational attainment, by region: 1984/5

Region	Percentage school-leavers with:	
	1 or more A-levels	*No graded results*
North	12.7	11.4
Tyne and Wear	11.2	12.3
Yorkshire and Humberside	13.2	10.5
South Yorkshire	11.9	10.3
West Yorkshire	12.0	12.1
East Midlands	13.3	8.5
East Anglia	12.4	9.1
South-east	16.3	9.4
Greater London	14.5	14.6
South-west	13.0	6.2
West Midlands	12.2	11.5
West Midlands (metropolitan area)	10.4	13.6
North-west	12.9	11.7
Greater Manchester	12.3	12.3
England	12.9	9.9
Wales	16.3	16.6
Scotland	30.7	25.8
Northern Ireland	22.4	22.4

Source: Central Statistical Office, *Regional Trends*, 1987.

obtaining five or more O-levels) according to factors such as occupational social group, ethnicity, and proportions of one-parent families for the child populations of local education authorities(LEA). On this basis, the Inner London Education Authority was ranked about average (56th out of 96 authorities). The ranking of authorities in Gray and Jesson's scheme did not show that inner urban areas had consistently better or worse achievement levels than elsewhere, nor did education spending by the authorities show a clear association with achievement. Although the means of standardization has its limitations, the study does show that the factors affecting educational outcomes are probably complex. The question of educational inequalities is given further attention in Chapters 4 and 6.

Inequalities in health

Over a long period social inequalities in health have been observed in the UK, and two reports have drawn attention to class differences in mortality and morbidity (Townsend, Davidson *et al.* 1988). The Black Report, produced at the beginning of the 1980s, showed that age- and sex-standardized mortality rates are higher for those from occupational group V than group I, especially for middle-aged men and for young children under 1 year (Townsend and Davidson 1982). The level of chronic illness (as indicated in the *General Household Survey*, for example) was also apparently higher among the manual classes (Walters 1981). Whitehead (1987, Townsend, Davidson *et al.* 1988) has concluded that since the Black Report was first published, in 1981, the mortality differentials have persisted between the social classes. The differences in prevalence of chronic illness reported in the *General Household Survey* had apparently increased for some age-groups between 1974 and 1984 (OPCS 1986b). The reasons for these disparities, and how far social inequalities in health may be widening, is open to debate (Townsend and Davidson 1982; Whitehead 1987; Aiach *et al.* 1988; Grand and Illsley 1987), but there seems little doubt that differences in health along class lines do exist in the UK.

Variations in rates of death and illness are also evident for geographical areas of the UK. These partly reflect demographic differences; they also relate to social class differences in life expectancy and the experience of illness. However, there do appear to be independent regional components in the variation of death rates, as shown in the analysis of regional mortality rates, controlling for social class differences reproduced in Table 1.5.

Fox, Jones, and Goldblatt (1984) have reported results from the

Table 1.5   Regional variations in mortality rates in England, adjusted for age and social class composition of the population: 1978

Region	Standardized mortality ratio, adjusted for population differences in:	
	Age	*Age and social class*
North	113	113
Yorkshire and Humberside	106	105
North-west	116	116
East Midlands	96	94
West Midlands	105	105
East Anglia	84	83
South-east	90	90
South-west	93	93

Source: Fox and Adelstein, 1978.

Longitudinal Study, a continuous longitudinal sample survey of people first selected from those enumerated in the 1971 population Census. Their findings show differences in mortality rates between types of area which are only partly explained by socio-economic class (Table 1.6). The broad pattern of health status in the UK appears to be for higher rates of ill-health and death in the north and west, and lower rates in the south and east, with comparatively poorer health status in urban as compared to rural areas.

Table 1.6   Standardized mortality rates for occupational groups in selected types of area

Type of area*	Standardized mortality ratios for occupational groups		
	I/II	*IIINM/IIIM*	*IV/V*
Residential retirement areas	80	85	93
New towns	66	97	111
Older industrial settlements	92	102	103
Inner urban areas with low-quality older housing	122	125	127

* Area clusters derived from Webber and Craig's Classification (1978).
Source: Fox *et al.*, 1984.

Inequalities in housing

Housing quality can be determined in terms of shelter, availability of household amenities, accessiblity to work, services and amenities, physical and social environment in the home, and the rights and obligations of occupancy (Bourne 1981). Rex (1971) showed that housing status could be categorized on the basis of these aspects of housing quality as shown in Table 1.7.

Those who generally enjoyed the best housing status were owner-occupiers, and those with the worst conditions on average were private sector tenants with absentee landlords. Public sector tenants, living in housing rented from local authorities, were in an intermediate position in the hierarchy. Varying housing class typifies different social groups, and different geographical areas.

Table 1.8 shows that the proportion of households who are living in owner-occupied accommodation varies between the occupational classes, being highest for those in the more privileged professional class. Proportionately more of the manual classes live in council rented

Table 1.7   Housing status categories and housing classes

Housing classes in rank order

---

1 (most privileged)	Outright owner
2	Owner under mortgage

3	Public sector tenant
	   (a) buildings with long life;
	   (b) buildings with short life

4	Tenant with absentee landlord
5	Tenant with landlord compelled to rent
6 (least privileged)	Tenant in rooming-house

Source: Rex, 1971, and Bourne, 1981.
Note: 'Housing status' is determined by: shelter; public utilities; amenities/access to work or services; environment (social and physical); and rights and obligations of occupancy.

housing. Variation in the proportion occupying privately rented housing shows a less clear pattern, perhaps because of the very variable quality of privately rented accommodation. The geographical distribution of housing tenure also varies, with a higher proportion of people in the north occupying council housing and more owner-occupiers in the south (Table 1.9).

Inequalities in access to private transport

Perhaps the most pertinent measure of access to transportation is car ownership, since lack of private transport can impose constraints on access and amenities, both in rural and urban settings. Access to private car transport is associated with socio-economic class, since car ownership is higher among the professional and managerial classes and lower among manual workers, especially the unskilled group (Table 1.10).

Indeed lack of a household car is often used as a surrogate measure of economic deprivation in the UK. Table 1.11 shows that the proportion of households without a car also varies by region, and is greatest in the north of the country and lowest in the south-west and south-east. In Chapter 5 it is argued that the provision of public transport services does not generally compensate fully for lack of

Table 1.8 Housing tenure of occupational groups in the UK: 1981

Occupational group of head of household (100%)	Owner occupied: outright	mortgaged	Rented from: employer	council	housing association/ co-operative	Privately rented: unfurnished	furnished
Professional	11	77	4	1	1	2	4
Employers/managers	17	68	4	8	<1	2	1
Intermediate non-manual	14	67	2	10	2	3	3
Junior non-manual	16	50	3	18	3	7	4
Skilled manual/own account	15	49	1	27	2	4	2
Semi-skilled manual/ personal service	13	30	5	41	3	4	4
Unskilled manual	13	23	<1	43	3	9	1
Economically inactive	24	35	2	29	2	5	2
All groups	24	35	2	29	2	5	2

The table header note: Percentage of households accommodated in housing which was:

Source: OPCS, 1985c, table 5.17.

Table 1.9   Housing tenure in regions of the UK: 1983

Region	Percentage of households in the region in accommodation which was:		
	Owner occupied	*Rented from local authority*	*Other rented property*
North	53	36	12
Yorkshire and Humberside	60	29	10
East Midlands	65	25	11
East Anglia	64	23	13
South-east	62	25	14
South-west	68	19	13
West Midlands	62	29	9
North-west	64	27	10
England	62	26	12
Wales	65	25	10
Scotland	38	53	9
Northern Ireland	57	35	8
UK	60	29	11

Source: Central Statistical Office, *Regional Trends*, 1983.

private transport, and those most in need of public transport are often least able to bear the costs of using it.

The geography of inequality

The descriptions above indicate two broad geographical dimensions of inequalities in wealth and welfare in the UK. One of these is the differences between the main conurbations and the rest of the country. This might be interpreted as an urban-rural division, although since Britain is predominantly an urbanized nation, it is perhaps more accurate to see it as an indication of the special situation in the highly urbanized inner cities. The second dimension of geographical variation is the north–south divide, which is becoming increasingly evident in terms of general health and well-being. The south of England (especially the south-east) is more privileged than the north in terms of several measures of health and well-being considered here. These divisions seem to reflect important spatial differences, in addition to the effect of the geographical distribution of socio-economic classes. Geographical inequalities are therefore complex phenomena.

19

Table 1.10   Occupational social class differences in car ownership
in Britain: 1984

Occupational group of head of household	Percentage of households in group lacking household car
Professional	5
Employer/manager	7
Intermediate/ junior non-manual	24
Skilled manual	21
Semi-skilled manual	46
Unskilled manual	62
Economically inactive	66
All groups	38

Source: OPCS, 1985c.

Table 1.11   Regional differences in car ownership

Region of residence	Percentage of households without a car
North	48
Yorkshire and Humberside	42
East Midlands	35
East Anglia	27
South-east	32
Greater London	43
South-west	28
West Midlands	40
North-west	44
Wales	34
Scotland	47
Northern Ireland	41
UK	37

Source: OPCS, 1987, p. 76.

If the objective of the welfare provision is to achieve a more equitable distribution of 'well-being' in British society, the existence of such inequalities brings into question the effectiveness of the public services (Le Grand 1982). The following chapters explore in more detail the varying levels of well-being in the UK space, and considers these in relation to the availability of public services for different social groups in different geographical localities.

The inequalities observed are the result of social and political processes which have an important geographical dimension. Pinch (1985) has discussed the tension betweeen social theories which stress the structure of society (especially Marxist and neo-Marxist interpretations) and those which place emphasis on the extent to which human behaviour influences the pattern of collective consumption (Weberian and related theory). Pinch proposes a framework which combines some elements of both views, suggesting that we should view the role of individual political and professional actors in the context of structural constraints. The most important of these are seen as external influences such as demography and market forces, and the role of local pressure groups and of central government. The relationship of these structural factors to patterns of local public welfare provision are discussed in the following chapters.

Chapter two

Administrative structures

Local authorities within the administrative system

The hierarchical structure of governmental administration in England and Wales is shown in Figure 2.1. At the top of the hierarchy, the heart of the political machine, is the Cabinet of officials representing the political party in power, and producing policy proposals which are subjected to the democratic process of parliamentary debate by elected Members of Parliament. Parliamentary legislation controls the activities of the civil service at the central and local level. The administration of society in the UK at the central level comprises central government departments. Those of particular interest to us here are the Department of the Environment (DoE), with responsibilities which include the allocation of central funds to local authorities for welfare provision, the Department of Health and Social Security (DHSS) (after 1988, the Department of Health) administering the National Health Service (NHS), the Department of Education and Science (DES) and the Department of Transport (DoT).

In addition to government departments, there are a large number of quasi-autonomous non-governmental organizations (QUANGOS), which include agencies such as the Manpower Services Commission(MSC), the Commission for Racial Equality(CRE), and the Equal Opportunities Commission(EOC). These are not directly controlled by government and are therefore independent, to some degree, of political change.

Local authorities are multi-purpose organizations which comprise the local tier of the structure, responsible for local government. They are elected bodies, with controlling members elected by the constituents of the local authority area. The functions of local authorities are limited by the legal principle of *ultra vires*, which prevents them from exceeding their statutory powers and responsibilities. Thus parliamentary legislation is important in determining what local authorities may do, as well as what they may

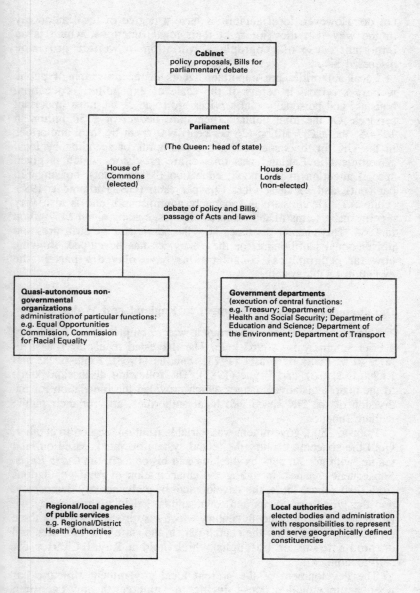

Figure 2.1 The administrative system in England

not do. However, local authorities have a degree of local autonomy in the way that they interpret their legal functions, which is an important cause of geographical variation in welfare provision discussed here.

Local authorities are important agents in the provision of public welfare services. In terms of the scale of expenditure, education, housing, and personal social services are some of the most important services. Of the total public expenditure budget of £130 billion in 1984/5, about £37 billion (26 per cent) was spent by local authorities in the UK. In the same year about two-thirds of spending by local government in England was on welfare provision, which is given special attention in this book; education (33 per cent), housing (25 per cent), and social services (7.5 per cent) (GB. Parliament, 1986, figure A1). Health care is separately administered, and is also very significant in terms of the resources it uses, costing about £17 billion in 1984. This chapter discusses how the administrative structures and jurisdictional partitioning for these services has developed, showing how far geographical considerations have played a part in the evolution of the system.

Development of local government in England and Wales

The development of local government was a complex process and only a brief summary is offered here. The interested reader may wish to refer to accounts by Fraser (1973), Smellie (1968), Keith-Lucas and Richards (1976), and Bryne (1983). The following discussion points to the main legislative changes which provided the foundation for the division of the UK space into local authorities, and for their public welfare functions.

Prior to 1800, government was variable from one region to another. Until the sixteenth century the feudal system operated, based on land tenure, with government by the king and his council, the *Curia Regis*. Subsequent changes, including the emancipation of rural populations from their feudal lords, the development of parliamentary democracy, and the growth of towns and town guilds, led to a structure by the beginning of the nineteenth century which comprised essentially three types of civil authority: the church parish, the shire in rural areas, and corporate towns or boroughs which held a Royal Charter for self-government.

The development of the present local government structure has been a piecemeal process during the nineteenth and twentieth centuries, begun in response to socio-economic changes associated with the Industrial Revolution. Bryne (1983: ch. 2) recognizes three phases of development; a period of stress and improvisation extending from 1800 to 1880, a phase of ascendancy of local authorities until 1930, and a period of decline since 1930.

Local authorities in the nineteenth century

Table 2.1 shows the important developments during the nineteenth century which provided the basis for the system existing until the 1970s. Before 1834, the parishes and towns had some responsibility to support the destitute, and this could be done by means of 'outdoor relief' – meagre benefits to the poor at home. Under the Poor Law Ammendment Act of 1834 poor relief for all except the old and sick was only to be provided in the workhouse, where conditions were to be less desirable than those of the lowest-paid worker in the community. Parishes were grouped into Unions, each with a workhouse, managed by a Board of Guardians, elected by ratepayers. Central administration was by the Poor Law Commission, set up under the Act, based in Somerset House in London, and comprising three salaried members, the 'pinch-pauper triumvirate', and a secretary. The Poor Law Ammendment Act was principally designed to reduce applications for poor relief, but it also introduced three principles of local government administration which were significant for the geography of public service provision. First, the Boards of Guardians were established as agencies with control over a particular service in a given area. Second, the Unions of parishes represented area groupings which were appropriate for the service being provided. Third, the principle of central administrative control over a locally organized service was established.

In 1835 the Municipal Corporations Act was the outcome of a Royal Commission on the government of towns, which examined the 178 Chartered Boroughs outside London. This was a response to the need for a better administrative system for the growing urban areas of an increasingly industrialized country. Corporate property, belonging to the borough, came under the control of an elected council. These councils were elected by the ratepayers, and had some functions in addition to control of municipal property: street maintenance, drainage, police, by-laws, and rate fixing and collection. Councils could appoint paid officials and were separated from the judicial system. Thus in urban areas elected councils acquired powers and responsibilities with respect to corporate property and some essential municipal services.

In the second half of the nineteenth century a series of legislative measures were passed by Parliament in response to increasing concern over public health issues, stimulated in part by the 'fever reports' and sanitary report produced by Chadwick and his colleagues (Chadwick

25

Table 2.1 Nineteenth-century developments in local government legislation (England and Wales)

Legislation	Structural changes	Effects on public administration
1834 Poor Law Amendment Act	Elected Board of Guardians for welfare provision in a given area; parishes united for Poor Law relief; central administration by Poor Law Board	Local public responsibility for welfare, areas for administration suited to a particular public service; principle of central control over a local service
1835 Municipal Corporations Act	Establishment of elected councils in chartered boroughs outside London	Corporate property and responsibility for some essential public services to elected councils representing local ratepayers
1848 Public Health Act	Created General Board of Health	A strong central body responsible for public health and local health boards
1871 Local Government Act	Created the Local Government Board combining functions of Poor Law Board, public health, Registrar-General	Combined responsibility for health and welfare (Poor Relief) functions to a single local body
1875 Public Health Act	Consolidated legislation during the 1870s and divided England and Wales outside London into urban and rural sanitary districts, supervised by the Local Government Board	Central control of local authorities through a government department; local responsibility for welfare and public health through elected representatives in urban districts
1888 Local Government Act	In the counties, administrative powers of JPs transferred to administrative county councils; each county had a council of representatives elected by ratepayers and counties were divided into equal-sized electoral districts; larger towns excluded from counties and given borough status; London administered through a metropolitan county	Elected local government representation in rural areas; division between urban and rural areas in administration
1894 Local Government Act	Local self-government for rural parishes by parish councils elected by ratepayers; local Boards of Health	Elected representation on rural parish councils; local government and welfare/public health

1842; Finer 1952; Lewis 1952), and spurred on by the threats posed by outbreaks of typhus and cholera in British cities. In 1848 the Public Health Act set up a General Board of Health, a central authority for public health, with power to establish local health districts. The 1871 Local Government Act created a Local Government Board, combining the functions of the Poor Law Board, public health administration, and the role of the Registrar-General (responsible for birth and death registration). Thus health and welfare functions began to be combined. The 1875 Public Health Act introduced urban and rural sanitary districts, a structure for local administration of health and welfare services (by elected representatives in urban areas), administered centrally through the Local Government Board.

In 1888 and 1894 two further pieces of legislation brought rural areas into line with the situation prevailing in the towns. In rural areas administration was hitherto the responsiblity of Justices of the Peace, responsible for functions such as fixing local taxes. The Local Government Act 1888 set up elected councils for rural areas, responsible for counties, which corresponded geographically to judicial quarter session court areas. These were divided into equal-sized electoral districts. The Local Government Act 1894 provided for elected councils to administer parishes, and converted urban and rural sanitary districts into district councils. The 1888 legislation had also created the County of London, and in 1899 this was subdivided into twenty-eight borough councils and the City of London.

This legislation thus gradually brought together public health and welfare functions, which became the responsibility of elected councils representing ratepayers in local areas, operating independently of the judicial administrative system. The structure existing by the end of the nineteenth century was not radically altered until the 1970s, except for changes of boundary and the establishment of the Greater London Council (see following section). Figure 2.2 shows this structure as it existed in 1971.

Twentieth-century evolution of local authorities

During the twentieth century pressure grew for further change in the welfare system, and some of the resulting legislation is summarized in Table 2.2. Several studies had shown that public welfare provision under the Poor Law was not adequate to meet the growing needs of deprived populations in some urban areas. Booth (1892) and Rowntree (1902) had demonstrated chronic poverty (see Chapter 1). The Royal Commission on the Poor Law and Relief of Distress through Unemployment (1905–9) recommended abolition of the Boards of

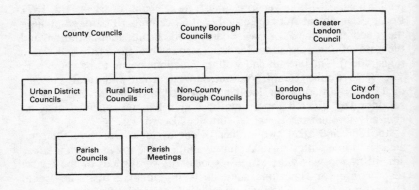

Figure 2.2 Local government before the 1974 local government act.
(Source: Bryne, 1983, p. 30)

Guardians and the workhouses and the introduction of a new system
of public assistance and labour exchanges to provide poor relief and
help to the unemployed, based on the perception that poverty was not
reprehensible. In Poplar, east London, two members of the local Board
of Guardians, Lansbury and Crooks, caused a political storm by giving
poor relief freely and refusing to pay the County of London rate
precept on the grounds that they did not receive any assistance from
wealthier parts of London to offset the costs of welfare provision. In
1929 the Local Government Act abolished Boards of Guardians,
established Public Assistance Committees in local authorities, and
introduced procedures for central government financial support to local
government funds, to help equalize the burden of expenditure, through
the Rate Support Grant (discussed in Chapter 7).

By the 1960s it was becoming evident that a revision of the
structure was needed for the local government of England and Wales
which, for areas outside London, had been in existence for over sixty
years. The Redcliffe-Maude Report on local government organization
(Great Britain. Parliament 1969a, 1969b) showed the main weaknesses
of the structure, using an analysis based in part on the geographical
ideas discussed in Chapter 1. It was found that local government areas
did not fit patterns of life and work in England. The system was too
fragmented and prevented effective planning. There were conflicts

Table 2.2 Some twentieth-century legislation relevant to local authorities in England and Wales

Legislation	Changes	Effects on local authorities
1929 Local Government Act	Abolished Boards of Guardians, introduced the rate support grant	Removal of Poor Law structures; introduction of redistribution of local government finance
1963 London Government Act	In response to the Herbert Commission report, GLC created with 32 London boroughs + city	Strategic planning body set up for London as a whole; the idea of a metropolitan agency
1972 Local Government Act	Reorganization of local government in response to the Redcliffe-Maude Report; set up non-metropolitan counties, metropolitan counties, and districts; revised responsibilities of local authorities	Organization on principles including social geography; metropolitan agencies, as well as districts, in main urban areas
1985 Local Government Act	Implemented the government report *Streamlining the Cities*; abolished GLC and metropolitan counties; metropolitan functions transferred to boroughs/ districts; some special agencies set up for Fire, Police, defence, transport (London)	Weakened intermediate level of administration, and removed directly elected regional planning agencies for large urban areas

between boroughs responsible for urban areas and counties concerned with their rural hinterlands. There was great disparity in size between local authorities, and several authorities were too small for efficient service provision. The Royal Commission recommended that local authority areas should be based on the interdependence of town and country; environmental services and personal social services should be in the hands of a single authority, and local authorities should be large enough to comprise common environmental interests and sufficient resources to provide services. A total of fifty-eight areas were suggested, ranging from 250,000 to 1,000,000 population, with very large areas divided up to maintain local accountability.

Thus the emphasis was on large unitary authorities, although in his dissenting memorandum, Derek Senior appealed for regard to the facts of social geography, and proposed smaller regional authorities for strategic functions and district councils for personal services of a more local nature.

The debate led to the 1972 Local Government Act, which was implemented in 1974, and brought a new structure, illustrated in Figure 2.3, with forty-seven county councils, subdivided into 333 district and borough councils, and thirty-six metropolitan district

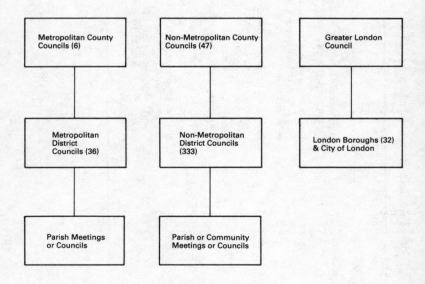

Figure 2.3 Local government after 1974 in England and Wales. (Source: Bryne, 1983, p. 53)

(a) ENGLAND AND WALES

Metropolitan Counties
Strategic planning;
traffic & transport
co-ordination;
passenger transport;
police; fire services;
refuse disposal;
consumer protection;
amenities.

Non-Metropolitan Counties
Strategic planning;
traffic & transport
co-ordination; police;
fire services;
education; libraries;
personal social
services; refuse
disposal; consumer
protection; amenities

Greater London Council
Strategic planning;
transport and some
housing services;
refuse disposal;
consumer protection;
amenities.

ILEA
Education in inner
London Boroughs

Metropolitan Districts
Education; libraries;
personal social
services; housing;
local planning;
environmental health;
leisure services &
local amenities

Non-Metropolitan Districts
Housing; local planning;
passenger transport;
environmental health;
leisure services.
In Wales, refuse disposal.

London Boroughs
Personal social
services; some
housing, leisure;
public health;
outer London Boroughs
responsible for
education.

**Local Councils
(Communities in Wales)**
Local amenities.

(b) SCOTLAND

Regions
Strategic planning; education;
social work; transport; water,
sewerage and flood protection;
police; fire services.

Island Areas
All regional
and district
functions

Districts
Housing; local planning;
local amenities; environmental health;
refuse collection & disposal; libraries;

Councils
Local amenities

(c) IRELAND

Central administration, with some regional devolution of functions such
as housing, transport, education and personal social services.
other functions carried out by District Councils.

Figure 2.4 Division of local government responsibilities for welfare
provision 1974–86 (partly based on Bryne, 1983, p. 68.)

31

councils, grouped into six metropolitan counties. The counties ranged in population from 10,000 in Powys to 1,500,000 in Hampshire. The metropolitan districts included populations varying from 173,000 in South Tyneside to 1,000,000 in Birmingham. The metropolitan counties were West Midlands (the largest with 2,700,000 people), Greater Manchester, South Yorkshire, West Yorkshire, and Tyne and Wear (the smallest with 1,000,000 population).

Under this system the division of welfare provision responsibilities is as shown in Figure 2.4. The main authority with responsibility for welfare provision in rural areas was the County, and in metropolitan areas the Metropolitan District. The Parish was retained as a local tier of government for grass-roots representation. The structure in London was not affected by these changes.

One of the criteria which the Royal Commission had considered in its proposals was the need to minimize disruption where possible by retaining old boundaries. This meant that in some parts of the country the changes in partitioning were not dramatic. However,in some cases the change was more significant; for example, the creation of the County of Avon in 1974 involved hiving off parts of Somerset and Gloucestershire to include the whole urban region of Bristol in the new unit (see Figure 2.5).

The rise and fall of metropolitan administration

Following the Herbert Commission, which examined local government in London (Great Britain. Parliament 1961), the Local Government Act 1963 created the Greater London Council (GLC). The functions of the GLC were examined in an inquiry chaired by Sir Frank Marshall, which reported in 1978. The report of this inquiry endorsed the view that some government functions, such as education (at least in inner London), housing, transport and fire protection, should be administered at least in part by a body which would represent all London authorities. Similarly, the Redcliffe-Maude Report had seen a need for a regional tier of government in other metropolitan areas to oversee planning, environmental services, and transport, and under the system existing until 1986, the GLC and metropolitan authorities all had the status of elected bodies accountable to the electorate of urban areas they covered.

However, the prevailing view of central government in the 1980s has been that the elected metropolitan authorities should go. It was argued in the White Paper, *Streamlining the Cities* (GB. Parliament 1983a), that the reorganizations of the 1960s and 1970s placed exaggerated confidence in strategic planning. Metropolitan authorities were not considered to have a clearly defined role between central

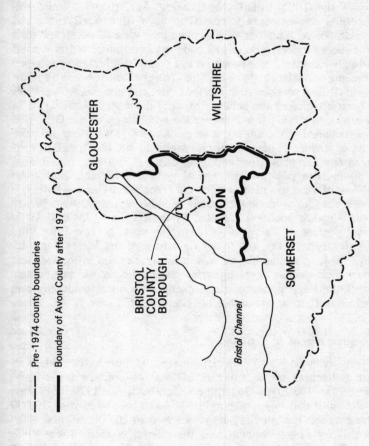

GLOUCESTER

WILTSHIRE

AVON

BRISTOL
COUNTY
BOROUGH

SOMERSET

Bristol Channel

——— Pre-1974 county boundaries

━━━ Boundary of Avon County after 1974

Figure 2.5 Boundary changes associated with the creation of Avon County in 1974

and local government. Borough and district councils were thought to be the appropriate geographic scales to represent the broad interests of urban populations, while still retaining accessibility to the community. Metropolitan authorities were also too costly, and in line with general cost cutting in the civil service, economies needed to be made.

Under the 1985 Local Government Act, the GLC and the metropolitan county councils ceased to exist from April 1986, and most metropolitan functions such as planning, waste disposal, and road and transport services (except in London), were transferred to district or borough councils. Some functions in London still had to be retained at the metropolitan level. The Inner London Education Authority(ILEA) persists as an elected body, and non-elected agencies have been established for police, fire, civil defence, and transport. In 1986 a residuary body to administer the winding-up of the GLC was all that remained of the unitary strategic authority for Greater London. The new structure places more emphasis on the local tier of government for provision and planning of services, but it also strengthens the position of central government, and limits the possibility of strategic planning for the conurbations as a whole.

These changes were implemented in spite of a strident publicity campaign against abolition mounted by the GLC in 1984 and 1985, featuring posters with slogans such as: 'Say no to no say: What kind of place is it that takes away your right to vote and leaves you with no say?' This campaign slogan was drawing attention to the fact that the new metropolitan level agencies are no longer elected bodies. Some of the implications of these changes for local autonomy and for public welfare provision are considered in Chapter 7.

Local government in Scotland

The long tradition and powerful status of burghs provided an important linchpin to the structure of local government in Scotland (Bryne 1983). The Local Government (Scotland) Act 1929 introduced a system with two types of burghs: 21 large burghs of over 20,000 inhabitants, and 176 smaller burghs of less than 20,000. In rural areas the local tier of government was the district council. These were organized into thirty-three county councils. The Wheatley Commission paralleled the Redcliffe-Maud Commission, and emphasized three criteria:

(1) functional viability;
(2) correspondence with community;
(3) democratic viability.

The Commission recommended a two-tier structure with seven

regional authorities and thirty-seven district authorities, and a very local tier of community councils where necessary. The Local Government (Scotland) Act 1973 brought into effect the structure shown in Figure 2.6; the functions of these authorities are shown in Figure 2.4.

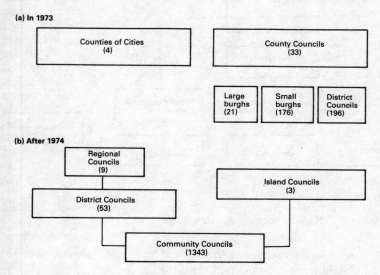

Figure 2.6 Scottish administrative structure. (Source: Bryne, 1983, p.63)

The National Health Service

Introduced in 1948, the National Health Service (NHS) was part of a new state welfare system designed to combat the five 'giants' of want, disease, ignorance, squalor, and idleness, identified by Beveridge (1942).

The original structure involved Hospital Boards, (concerned with hospital medicine), Local Health Authorities (municipal community health agencies), and Executive Councils (administering services provided by family practitioners). After reorganization of the health service in 1974, a new structure was introduced, with Regional Health Authorities, Area Health Authorities, and District Health Authorities. Further changes in 1982 removed the area tier (see Figure 2.7).

As in the case of local authority organization, the NHS structure has a hierarchical arrangement with important geographical elements. Successive changes in the administrative structure have tried to strike a balance between the following:

35

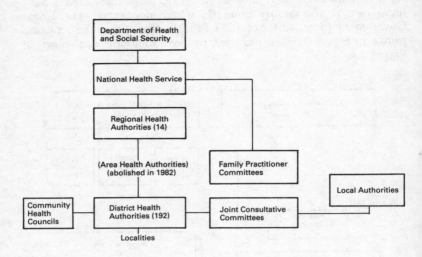

Figure 2.7 National health structure since 1982

(1) social geography (settlement and transport patterns, established community identities);
(2) the appropriate geographical range and catchment population of hospitals (e.g. 200,000–500,000 suggested for a district general hospital);
(3) the need for collaboration and coterminosity with local government administrations.

Scotland and Northern Ireland do not have Regional or District Health Authorities. In Scotland, at an intermediate scale, there are fifteen Health Boards (Mair 1983). Northern Ireland is the only part of the UK where health and social service adminstration is unified under four Health and Social Services Boards (Haynes 1987: ch. 1).

Geographical elements in the evolution of the public welfare system

Over time there have been changes in the prevailing view of what is the most appropriate way of organizing welfare provision. The British case shows, for example, the variable emphasis placed on the need for a regional tier of administration for public services. Elements of social geography which, as we have seen, are significant for jurisdictional partitioning and the allocation of responsibilities to different levels of the public service hierarchies, have often featured in the debates over local government organization. Geographical division of the national space for the administration of welfare will influence the availability and accessibility of public services to clients in different localities, and the effect of this on particular types of consumers is considered in more detail in later chapters; the controversies over political questions of local accountability and autonomy are also important, and these are returned to in Chapter 7.

Chapter three

The administrative geography of the major welfare services

Welfare services as spatial systems

This chapter focuses on health and personal social services, education, housing, and transport – those parts of the welfare system which receive most attention in this book. Responsibilities of local authorities for these aspects of welfare provision are very wide-ranging, and it is not proposed to discuss all of them in detail here. Certain aspects of welfare provision are selected for particular attention because of their significance to the client groups discussed later in the book, and because of their geographical dimensions which are of interest here. For a detailed compendium of the provision of these services, the reader is directed to the text by Bryne and Padfield (1985). In this chapter the historical development of responsibilities for welfare provision are considered, to show how trends in national and local policies influence the geography of public welfare provision. The British case provides an interesting example of how public welfare services evolve in response to social and political changes in society.

The powers and responsibilities of local agencies with respect to these services affect the geographical distribution of services across the country. Provision of these services to meet the welfare needs of the population often requires co-ordination between agencies which are administratively separate, with differing spatial organization. Questions of spatial coterminosity of jurisdictional areas, and of spatial distribution of facilities, are important to co-ordination between agencies and the accessibility of care for the population. We may consider the provision of these services using the paradigms first made popular in geography by writers such as Haggett (1968) and Massam (1975) in terms of a number of interrelated spatial systems, comprising divisions of the UK space into adminstrative units and nodes for service delivery.

Personal social services

Personal social services include a range of services for different types of client. Examples include domiciliary and residential services for frail, elderly people; care of children, especially those deprived of a normal home life; and services for handicapped people, or for cultural groups with special needs. These became the responsibility of the social service departments of local authorities, created in 1971, following the proposals of the Seebohm Committee (Great Britain. Parliament 1968a). The administrative areas within which personal social services are provided therefore correspond to local authority boundaries (non-metropolitan counties, metropolitan districts, and London boroughs). The Social Service Departments (SSDs) are controlled by democratically elected councils. For operational and management purposes, local authority areas are often subdivided into social service divisions or 'patches'. Where local authority organization is decentralizing to 'neighbourhoods' (for example, in Islington and Tower Hamlets in London), these smaller units may form the basis for much of the administration and provision of social care.

Social workers are key professionals, and the Seebohm proposals, implemented in the Local Authority Social Services Act, 1970, introduced the idea of the generic social worker, and resulted in the amalgamation of previously separate local authority departments concerned with services for children, welfare, and health, to form the new social service departments.

At present, there is an increasing trend towards the provision of some forms of social care through the private and voluntary sectors. This applies, for example, to residential services for the elderly, discussed in Chapter 5.

Health services

The National Health Service (NHS), under the present system of organization, provides medical care in hospitals and in the community. The administrative structure of the NHS, summarized in Figure 2.7, has been subject to changes and discussion about the most appropriate geographical organization of the service. In 1968 a Green Paper on the administrative structure of medical and related services in England and Wales (DHSS 1968) proposed combining Executive Councils and Regional Hospital Boards, together with local authorities, into a single authority, the Area Board, of which there would be forty or fifty in the UK. In 1970 an alternative strategy was suggested (DHSS 1970), with about ninety area health authorities (AHAs), corresponding to the local authority areas proposed by the Redcliffe-Maud Commission (see

Chapter 2). This second Green Paper also recommended regional health authorities (RHAs) to co-ordinate provision of health care at the wider geographical scale, and district health authorities (DHAs) to provide care at the local level. This was the structure eventually adopted. Unlike the social service departments, NHS authorities are not responsible to a democratically elected council.

In 1982 further legislation in response to the Royal Commission on the NHS (Great Britain. Parliament 1979b) removed the AHA tier of the administration, leaving a system with RHAs and DHAs. This removal of the area tier of the health service was argued, by some observers, to be detrimental to co-ordination between health and social services because it removed the geographical zones in the NHS which most naturally corresponded with local government boundaries in some parts of the country (Harbridge 1981). Joint Consultative Committees (JCCs) are intended to provide the necessary link between the NHS at district level and the local authorities to ensure co-ordinated welfare provision to those in need.

General practitioner services remain a notably separate part of the structure. Family Practitioner Committees (FPCs) administer these services, together with practitioners such as dentists and opticians, and are responsible for geographical areas corresponding to the now defunct AHAs. General practitioners themselves are contracted to the NHS, rather than being employees of the service, and the controls exercised over their activities by the FPCs are quite limited.

There is an increasing trend, similar to that in local authorities, towards the planning and co-ordinating of services at a very local level ('patch' or 'locality' planning). Health care of the population living in the community should be co-ordinated through primary health care teams, comprising community nurses, health visitors, general practitioners, and other community health professionals. The view of the Cumberlege Report on community nursing in England (DHSS 1986a), endorsed in the 1987 White Paper on primary health care (GB. Parliament 1987a), was that the primary health care team is well placed to respond to the local needs of particular communities because of their close contact and knowledge of the locality, and that community services should be organized and managed at this neighbourhood level of operation. Typical neighbourhoods were envisaged as having 10,000–25,000 people. This patch or locality planning and management of health care is becoming increasingly common in DHAs throughout the UK, although the model of patch planning being adopted is rather variable, determined according to local circumstances.

Another notable trend in the provision of health care is the considerable growth of the private sector. The restraints imposed on

NHS finance in recent years are discussed in Chapter 7, and they have been accompanied by an expansion of commercial and non-profit-making private medicine, especially in hospital provision. The geographical distribution of the private medical sector is uneven across the country, and is particularly focused in the south-east. This is partly because the private sector develops most successfully alongside the NHS hospitals (Mohan 1985; Griffiths, Raynor, and Mohan 1985; Mohan and Woods 1985), and also because those able to afford private medical insurance are concentrated particularly in the outer urban zone surrounding London (OPCS 1983a).

Division of responsibilities for health and social care: a continuing debate

Figures 3.1 and 3.2 show the community health and welfare responsibilities of local authorities before and after the administrative changes of the 1970s. Comparison of the two figures will show that local authorities previously had more responsibility for community health functions, and the functions transferred to the NHS from local authorities in 1974 included community health surveillance, preventative health care, ambulance services, health centres, and health visiting and domiciliary nursing.

The allocation of responsibilities for health and social services has been the subject of continuing debate. Both the Seebohm Report and the Royal Commision on the Health Service, chaired by Sir Alec Merrison (Great Britain. Parliament 1979b) concluded that responsibility for health and social services should rest with separate authorities.

Alternative arrangements which were considered for health and social services in the Merrison Report (ch. 16) included:

(1) transfer of NHS functions to local authorities;
(2) transfer of personal social services to the NHS;
(3) transfer of responsibility for client groups (e.g. the NHS should take sole responsibility for elderly people, while SSDs would be responsible for those with mental handicap).

The first option was favoured by groups such as the Association of County Councils because it offered unified responsibility for complementary services, and would facilitate comprehensive planning. Although health care is a major undertaking, it was considered no more difficult or expensive than the education services already managed by the local authorities. Such a system would allow for direct accountability of the health service to the electorate, and might make

41

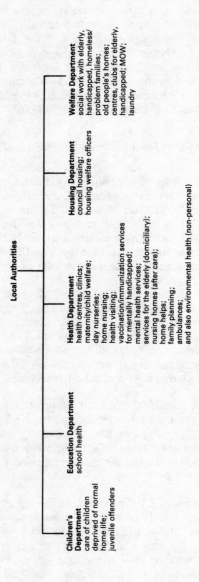

Local Authorities

Children's Department
care of children deprived of normal home life;
juvenile offenders

Education Department
school health

Health Department
health centres, clinics;
maternity/child welfare;
day nurseries;
home nursing;
health visiting;
vaccination/immunization services for mentally handicapped;
mental health services;
services for the elderly (domiciliary);
nursing homes (after care);
home helps;
family planning;
ambulances;
and also environmental health (non-personal)

Housing Department
council housing;
housing welfare officers

Welfare Department
social work with elderly, handicapped, homeless/problem families;
old people's homes;
centres, clubs for elderly, handicapped; MOW;
laundry

Figure 3.1 Community health and social service functions of local authorities: 1968

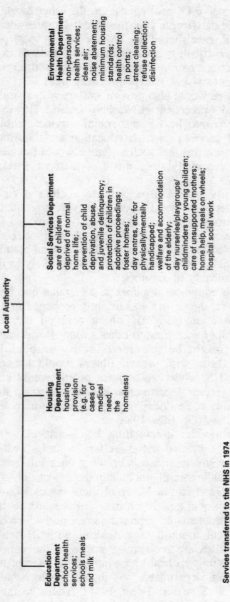

Local Authority

Education Department
school health services;
schools meals and milk

Housing Department
housing provision
(e.g. for cases of medical need, the homeless)

Social Services Department
care of children deprived of normal home life;
prevention of child deprivation, abuse, and juvenile delinquency;
protection of children in adoptive proceedings;
foster homes;
day centres, etc. for physically/mentally handicapped;
welfare and accommodation of the elderly;
day nurseries/playgroups/childminders for young children;
care of unsupported mothers;
home help, meals on wheels;
hospital social work

Environmental Health Department
non-personal health services;
clean air;
noise abatement;
minimum housing standards;
health control in ports;
street cleaning;
refuse collection;
disinfection

Services transferred to the NHS in 1974
community health surveillance;
ambulance services;
family planning;
health centres;
health visiting;
domiciliary nursing/midwifery;
preventative health care;
care and after care of the sick

Figure 3.2 Division of responsibilities for health and welfare after 1971

health care more responsive to local needs. On the other hand, it was seen as a threat to clinical freedom by the medical professions, who would argue that health care should not be involved in local politics. It would make it more difficult to achieve national standards in health care. Some health functions require regional planning, and no regional tier of local government existed, except in urban areas.

The second alternative would also provide unitary responsibility for allied services, and had a precedent in Northern Ireland. However, the result would be to separate health and social services from other important and related services such as education and housing. The social workers were concerned that such a change would threaten their professional freedom, especially since much of their work relates to non-medical problems.

The final possibility would also provide a clear division of responsibility for clients of different types. However, it seemed likely that similar types of professional would need to be employed in both services. In some cases, it would be difficult to categorize clients, especially where socio-medical problems involved several members of the same family. Financing of such a system seemed likely to involve a good deal of cross-subsidy of services.

In the face of these equivocal arguments, the status quo has until now prevailed. However, the debate was recently reopened in a report by the Audit Commission (1987a), which revived the idea of allocation of responsibility according to client group. It was suggested that elderly clients might be provided for by a special joint management group. Those with mental illness would become the responsibility of the NHS, while handicapped people would be cared for through the social service departments. Recent discussion has also focused on the possibility of reallocating responsibility for community health to local authorities (Griffiths 1988).

Another development which is refuelling the discussion over statutory responsibility for health and social welfare is the growth of the New Public Health Movement, which is bringing back into the public eye questions about public health, including the effects of housing, environmental hygiene, and so on. Many of these issues would have seemed familiar to the pubic health reformers of the last century. In order to address these problems an approach is required which extends beyond strictly medical methods for dealing with ill-health. In response, local authorities are reclaiming a role in the community health field, and are setting up health committees to attempt the sort of co-ordination between departments and agencies which has often been lacking in the NHS sector (Fryer 1987). There seems to be mounting pressure to review the division of responsibilities in the field of health, and for local authorities to play a more influential part.

The geography of co-ordination of health and social care

Under the existing system the provision of medical and social care to clients in need requires co-operation between local authorities and the NHS. For example, sick elderly people may need NHS care in hospital or by domiciliary nurses, but also SSD provision by hospital social workers, or home helps. Children may need both health surveillance and education services, and may also require medical treatment for illness or social work intervention in cases of families in difficulties.

How best to achieve co-ordination between social services and health services has been the subject of much debate. This is a particularly serious problem at a time when the emphasis in health policy is on a transfer of resources from the hospitals and institutions to care in the community. For the present, the only statutory administrative provision for co-ordinating services are the Joint Consultative Committees and the Joint Care Planning Teams. The first are responsible for developing co-ordinated plans for integrated health and social care. Since 1977 the NHS has allocated funds for finance of collaborative initiatives between health and social services, and this is allocated to projects by the JCCs. The total funding to joint finance has increased from about £30 million in 1978/9 to £90 million in 1983/4, but it remains less than 1 per cent of the total health care budget. The level of expenditure of joint finance moneys varies considerably between different parts of England, and is greatest in London (Table 3.1).

The Joint Care Planning Teams (JCPT) comprise health and social care professionals who liaise together to provide co-ordinated services for particular client groups. Arguably, these teams are the most crucial groupings in terms of the nature and quality of joint provision and, in some cases, their membership includes representatives of the private and voluntary sectors involved in provision of health and social services locally. The extent of development of joint planning has been found to vary considerably in different areas of the UK. There were particularly wide disparities in the development of subgroups of JCPTs with responsibility for specific client groups, which were considered the most effective form of collaboration. In 1982, in London, 46 per cent of area health authorities had not established JCPT subgroups, compared with 19 per cent of other metropolitan AHAs and 13 per cent of AHAs in the shire counties (Wistow and Fuller 1986). The National Audit Office (1987) has commented on the fact that joint planning is generally less well established than had been hoped.

One of the reasons for this slow development was identified as a problem of geographical mismatch of areas of responsibility for the agencies involved. The problem is well illustrated in London, where

45

Table 3.1 Expenditure of joint finance in different areas in England and Wales: 1985/6

	Total expenditure (£000s)	Total population	Expenditure (£000s)/ 1000 population
London boroughs	30,770	6,767,500	4.5
Metropolitan districts	28,564	11,201,300	2.6
Non-metropolitan districts	70,876	31,954,700	2.2
All authorities	130,210	49,923,500	2.6

Source: Chartered Institute of Public Finance and Accountancy; Personal Social Services Statistics; Actuals and OPCS Monitor PP1 86/2.

some of the health district boundaries cut across boroughs, as shown in Figure 3.3. Health authorities, such as Bloomsbury, Lewisham and North Southwark, Riverside and Paddington, and North Kensington, cut across borough boundaries and find themselves having to liaise with more than one local authority.

In areas where decentralization is well advanced the jurisdictional areas of the smaller health and social service localities will also be significant for the integration of services. In Tower Hamlets, in London, local authority neighbourhoods number seven, while four health authority patches are being proposed (Figure 3.4). While the boundaries of the health authority zones correspond to some of the boundaries of the local authority neighbourhoods, the personnel in the health patches will in many cases need to collaborate with more than one neighbourhood committee for social services. Neighbourhoods sometimes vary in their political persuasions, and their policies with respect to social care.

Thus the geographical considerations in the organization of health and social services are clear: questions of the appropriate catchment areas for services, of coterminosity of service areas, of decentralization of responsibilities or central control, and of political geography, have all contributed to the existing structures. Of course, geographical factors are not the only issues involved; for example, distributions of facilities and responsibilities owe much to historical social and political factors – see Rivett's (1986) account of the development of London's hospital system. Relationships between the different caring professions and their varying responsibilities and objectives (Packman 1975), and differences in ideologies of care and accountability to the public, also have an influence. Nevertheless, geographical aspects of

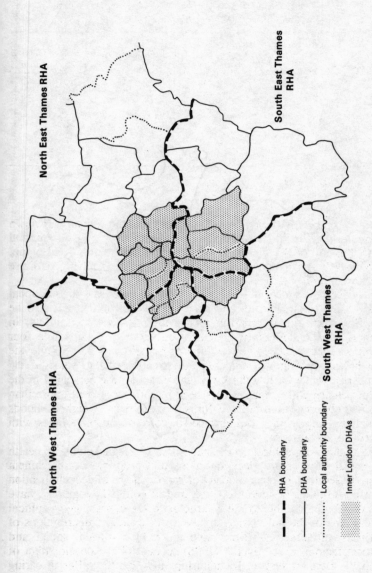

North East Thames RHA

North West Thames RHA

South East Thames RHA

South West Thames RHA

RHA boundary

DHA boundary

Local authority boundary

Inner London DHAs

Figure 3.3 District health authority and local authority (London borough) boundaries in London

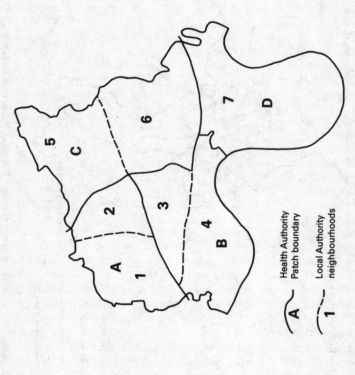

Figure 3.4 Local authority neighbourhood boundaries and proposed health authority patches in Tower Hamlets, London: 1987

the system remain important to the functioning of the health and social services and affect the nature and accessibility of health and social care for users (Joseph and Phillips 1984; Eyles and Woods 1983; Haynes 1987). These factors are further considered in the following chapters.

The organization of education

Education is administered centrally through the Department of Education and Science (DES), and locally by local education authorities (LEAs). The services provided by LEAs include compulsory full-time education for 5–16-year-olds, nursery education, courses in colleges of further education, financial support to students in universities and polytechnics, and adult education courses.

The precursors of the LEAs were the School Boards, set up under the Education Act of 1870. This Act divided the country into school districts, and granted the School Boards power to levy rates and provide schools. School attendance could be made compulsory between the ages of 5 and 13 years.

The Education Act of 1902 replaced the School Boards with LEAs which could themselves provide schools, or contribute to voluntary schools from the rates in return for representation in the management of these schools; the LEAs could also provide teacher training. The Central Board of Education was to provide central government funding to LEAs, and the new structure represented a national education system. Under the 1918 Education Act, LEAs were to provide free compulsory elementary education for children aged 5–13, and higher education for those over 13 wishing to stay on at school was to be provided, although fees could be charged.

Wider responsibilities and powers for LEAs were laid down under the Education Act of 1944. This strengthened central administration in the form of the Ministry of Education, and changed the organization of education. Schools were now divided according to their function, and LEAs were obliged to ensure adequate provision in primary schools for those under 11 years, secondary schools for those aged 11–15, and further education after the new legal school-leaving age of 15 (later raised to 16). Children were to be educated with regard to their 'age, abilities and aptitudes' and 'in accordance to the wishes of parents', in so far as these could be met efficiently and at reasonable cost. The 'dual system' of state schools and LEA-subsidized voluntary schools was retained. Although compulsory education does not begin until children reach 5 years, LEAs are required under the 1944 Act to provide nursery education where necessary.

The LEAs are empowered to provide additional services to promote the welfare of schoolchildren. These include clothing, school medical inspections, and assistance with transport to school. Until 1980, LEAs also provided school meals and milk to schoolchildren, but under the 1980 Education Act these can be provided free of charge only on grounds of ill-health or poverty.

The LEAs also have responsibilities for further education (beyond the age of 16) and higher (advanced) education which takes place outside the normal school classes. Further education includes adult education such as non-vocational evening classes; higher education is organized in a binary system, divided between the universities, independent bodies funded separately by the DES through the University Grants Council, and the polytechnics and colleges of further education, funded and administered by LEAs. The LEAs also provide grants to students for higher education in universities and other educational institutions.

Under the local government system existing in 1987 the LEAs are the non-metropolitan counties, the metropolitan districts, and in outer London, the London boroughs. For inner London, the Inner London Education Authority (ILEA) persisted in the period immediately after abolition of the GLC as the agency responsible for education in the capital. However, the Education Bill before Parliament in 1988 makes provision for the abolition of the ILEA, replacing this joint education authority by separate borough education departments.

Education provision raises several issues of particular interest for geographers because they bear upon the geographical variability of access to education of different types. One of these questions is whether LEAs should provide a fully 'comprehensive' education system, or whether there should be a greater range of choice between alternative types of education, and selection of children for different types of school; this is considered in the following section. A second important issue concerns the variability of LEA provision of education for children under compulsory schoolage. This relates to availability of nursery education for young children in different parts of the country. This question is discussed in Chapter 4, where we are concerned with provision to children and their families. In addition, the issue of positive discrimination in education to compensate disadvantaged children, and especially the concentration of resources into Educational Priority Areas raises questions about the effectiveness of area-based planning, which are also given attention in Chapter 4.

Access to education: selection, choice, and the role of the LEA

Under the organization introduced by the 1944 Act the selection procedure for non-comprehensive education took place at the age of 11, with the '11-plus examination', on the basis of which children were provided places either in the LEA-subsidized grammar schools or in secondary schools where the average academic standard tended to be lower, and there was less emphasis on acquiring academic qualifications and continuation to university. In 1964 the Ministry of Education was replaced by the Department of Education and Science, and in 1965 the department issued a Circular to LEAs declaring the government's objective to eliminate the 11-plus selection and the division in secondary education. All children were to enter the 'comprehensive' school for their area at 11 years, without selection. Over the following two years they would be streamed into 'sets' in appropriate subjects according to teachers' assessments.

There are several arguments in support of a comprehensive system. In terms of social geography and the social objectives of education, the system would provide for greater territorial equality in educational opportunity, and would help to break down barriers to social mobility. From the educational point of view, the 11-plus examination is questionable as a valid discriminator of children's later academic potential, and does not allow for subsequent movement between schools or streams of different standards. The system might have beneficial effects for pupils from learning in a mixed-ability situation, partly because the situation would be likely to be attractive to higher-calibre teachers wishing to teach the most able, as well as less able, students. The comprehensive schools would be larger and would therefore provide opportunities for economies of scale and a wider range of educational activities. Those not in favour of comprehensive education argue that schools should not be instruments of social reform and that, in any case, the benefits are theoretical and could be achieved without the introduction of comprehensive education. Good comprehensive schools need high standard, purpose-built facilities, and high-calibre staff, but inevitably there is some variation from one area to another in the quality of schools, due in part to historical distribution of facilities. It is suggested that, under a comprehensive system, the more privileged groups, who are most adept at manipulating the system, move to areas where the comprehensive schools are of higher standards, leaving less good schools with a catchment of less privileged families, unmotivated and ill-equipped to exert pressure for improvement, so that the geographical and social inequalities in education persist. There is argued to be a continuing need for less academic, more vocational training in schools, which

51

old-style secondary modern schools provided effectively. At the same time, the comprehensive system would be achieved at the expense of good grammar schools, producing a lowering in academic standards of education in the UK.

The issue of comprehensive education therefore has strong socio-political overtones, and has been described by Jackson (1976: 197) as a 'political shuttlecock', which has seen rapid reversals of central government policy according to the political persuasion of the party in power. By 1968 the majority of LEAs had submitted plans for reorganization of schools along comprehensive lines, although seven had refused to do so. In 1970 the new Conservative government withdrew the 1965 Circular, and restored the freedom of LEAs to choose the method of organization. Again, four years later the DES under a new Labour administration, issued a directive for LEAs to introduce comprehensive education since only about twenty authorities had so done completely. The Education Act 1976 brought in legislation designed to force recalcitrant LEAs to comply since some were still resisting the pressure to bring in a comprehensive system. Once again, the tide turned in 1979 when the Conservatives came back into power, and under the Education Act 1980, local authorities are again free to operate selective secondary education. The 1980 Act requires LEAs to be more responsive to parents' preferences, and to involve parents in determining schools' policies to a greater degree. Thus policies of schools, and the prevailing weight of local public opinion, are likely to influence the quality and accessibility of education for children in different parts of the UK.

Therefore, it is clear that central government policy plays an important role in deciding how much freedom LEAs can exercise in providing different types of education for different students. There are tendencies toward a more centralized education system. The Education Reform Act, passed in 1988, introduced greater central control over the syllabus in schools since schools might have to demonstrate that they were reaching the required standards in the core subjects. This implied a change in the professional independence of teachers in state schools. The legislation also allowed that schools might have the choice to opt out of LEA control. Under the new Act LEAs no longer have full control over school budgets or the allocation of pupils to schools. Parents may exercise individual choice in selecting schools for their children, and schools may compete to attract pupils. The LEA controls over the numbers of staff recruited are to be relaxed, so that more variable pupil–teacher ratios may be likely, depending on the ability of individual schools to pay staff costs, either through income support from the state or through additional voluntary parental contributions.

Education is thus a good example of a service which demonstrates the sometimes conflicting relationships between central and local policies for welfare provision. The present trends are tending to undermine LEA control, which is being vested increasingly in central government on the one hand, and with individual parents on the other hand. The resulting pattern of educational provision is likely to show greater variety in response to the policies of schools and of parent bodies involved in their management. Geographical differences in the nature and quality of education are likely to increase, and it seems reasonable to suppose that they will be best in areas where at present the local schools have a good reputation and where local parents are highly motivated and interested in achieving a high level of education for their children. The evidence we have discussed in Chapter 1 shows that these are likely to be those areas with a more privileged and highly educated population. It is true that the present system of education has apparently failed to remove social and geographical inequalities in access to education. However, it seems likely that these inequalities will increase under the new system that is proposed. The implications of geographical variations in education provision for children and their families are discussed in Chapter 4.

Local authorities and housing provision

Some of the factors contributing to housing quality and the housing status of different groups in the population have been considered already in Chapter 1. Local authorities play a role in determining access to housing because of their wide range of functions associated with housing (see Bryne and Padfield 1985, and Balchin 1985, for a more comprehensive description). In this book particular attention is given to the activities of local authorities with respect to provision and allocation of housing, and funding of housing improvement.

Balchin (1985: 157–9) has pointed out that at certain periods during this century local authorities have been seen to have a role in helping to alleviate a general housing shortage. However, at other periods (as at present), the local authorities have been restricted to a more marginal 'welfare role', providing for those who are homeless or in inadequate housing. The Housing Act, passed by Parliament in 1988, is intended to give effect to proprosals outlined in the White Paper, *Housing: The Government's Proposals* (GB. Parliament 1987b). The main aims of this legislation are to expand home ownership and to revitalize the private rented housing sector, while encouraging local authorities to change their housing role. The government wishes to see local authorities reducing their involvement as landlords, and increasingly taking on the role of 'enablers to ensure that everybody is adequately housed but not necessarily by them' (ibid.). Another plank of Conservative housing policy is the sale of council houses; thus what had come to be seen as the traditional role of the local authority, providing housing for a large proportion of the population for fair rents, is likely to alter radically as the proposals are brought into effect. The following sections consider the development of the local authority housing departments.

Local authority contributions to the housing stock

Local authorities began to contribute significantly to housing construction in the UK after the passing of the Housing and Town Planning Act 1919, which provided central government funds to support council house construction in the campaign to build 'homes fit for heroes' after the First World War. The amount of funding to local authorities was reduced after 1921, but between 1919 and 1930, 1,500,000 new council homes were built, providing a 20 per cent increase in the national housing stock over the period. Subsidies were ended in 1933, but the Housing Act 1946 reintroduced them as part of a reconstruction drive after the Second World War. In 1950 the public sector produced 184,400 new houses, representing almost ten times the number produced in the private sector. In 1955, although the private sector contribution had grown considerably, the public sector still provided 185,000 homes. Between 1960 and 1970 the number of new housing starts in the public sector never fell below 120,000 (Balchin 1985: 34).

At present the scale of the public sector housebuilding programme has been reduced. Balchin (pp.158–9) showed the reduction in new house starts by local authorities from 173,800 in 1975 to 80,100 in 1979 and 37,000 in 1981. Although the rate of public sector building began to rise again thereafter, it still had not gained pre-1978 levels. This reduction of local authority construction has occurred in spite of large numbers of homeless people; 93,980 households were registered homeless nationally in 1985 (Association of Metropolitan Authorities 1986). Under the Housing (Homeless Persons) Act 1977 local authorities must provide help and advice to homeless people, and must provide housing to those in priority groups such as families with children, pensioners, and the disabled, who are unintentionally homeless.

Where suitable housing is not otherwise available, the authority must pay bed-and-breakfast charges for temporary accommodation. This cost approximately £500 million in 1984, to house 163,000 families according to an article in the *Independent* newspaper, which condemned the practice as 'economic lunacy' in view of the high costs of bed-and-breakfast accommodation. It has been estimated that it costs £13,150 a year to provide a family with bed and breakfast in London, but that the initial cost of a loan to build a permanent home would amount only to £7,380 in the first year (*Independent*, 21 October 1986). The scale of such need to provide for homeless people varies between local authorities; it is particularly acute in the inner cities.

In part, the pressures on local authority housing are reflected by the variation in numbers of registered homeless persons recorded for different parts of the country (Table 3.2). The areas where local authorities or the private sector are most active in new homebuilding are not always those where the registered homeless population is largest. The greatest pressure is in the London area, where in 1983 the number of new dwellings completed by the private and public sectors combined was less than the number of homeless families accepted on to local authority registers (Table 3.2) and 32 per cent of new lettings by local authorities were to homeless families.

Local authorities also contribute to the housing stock through their programmes of slum clearance and housing renewal, which are particularly concentrated in the decaying inner cities. In the 1950s and 1960s local authorities were active in slum clearance and reconstruction. The 1956 Housing Subsidies Act restricted subsidies to projects for clearance, rehousing of urban overspill, and construction of small one-bedroom homes, thus giving priority to these types of development. Some of the redevelopment took the form of high-rise blocks, which changed the face of the urban landscape in many cities in the UK, and had important effects on the social functions of communities (Young and Willmott 1957; Cornwell 1984: ch. 2; Littlewood and Tinker 1981).

The tide of opinion in housing policy was turning by the late 1960s against clearance and replacement of housing with such developments, and swung towards refurbishment and renewal. The Parker Morris Committee (Central Housing Advisory Committee 1961) and the 1968 White Paper, *Old Houses into New Homes* (GB. Parliament 1968b), both advocated an emphasis on improvement, and the Housing Act 1969 increased the amount which local authorities might grant to private home owners towards the cost of home improvements. The authorities were empowered to designate General Improvement Areas (GIAs) where they could claim central government grants towards environmental improvement, as well as improvement grants to owners. The GIA scheme was revised under the Housing Act 1974, which introduced Housing Action Areas (HAAs), to be defined in terms of criteria including social stress (multiple occupation and shared amenities, low income, and high unemployment), as well as poor

55

Table 3.2 Population registered homeless, waiting-lists for council housing and new housing starts in regions of the UK

Region	New dwellings completed in 1983 per 1,000 population			Homeless households accepted by local authorities 1982/3	
	Private	Public	Total	No.	No./1,000 population
North	1.9	1.0	2.9	6,490	2.1
Yorkshire and Humberside	2.3	0.8	3.1	5,810	1.2
East Midlands	3.0	1.2	4.2	4,350	1.3
East Anglia	4.2	1.2	5.3	1,760	0.9
South-east	2.5	0.9	1.6	36,090	2.1
Greater London	0.7	0.9	1.6	24,050	3.6
Rest of SE	3.7	0.9	4.6	12,040	1.2
South-west	3.7	0.8	4.6	5,860	1.3
West Midlands	2.4	0.8	3.2	9,340	1.8
North-west	1.9	1.0	2.9	8,540	1.3
England	2.6	0.9	3.5	78,240	1.7
Wales	1.8	0.8	2.6	4,515	1.6
Scotland	2.5	0.9	3.4	7,531	1.5
Northern Ireland	2.3	2.9	5.2	n.a.	n.a.
United Kingdom	2.5	1.0	3.5		
Great Britain				90,286	1.7

Source: Central Statistical Office, *Regional Trends*, 1983.

physical condition of housing and problems of 'planning blight'. The main form of intervention was in the form of improvement grants of 75–90 per cent of the costs of renovation. Although it had been anticipated that 1 million dwellings would be covered by HAAs by 1980, in fact there were only 150,000 homes nationally in 546 HAAs; HAAs are particularly concentrated in London, Liverpool, Birmingham, and Manchester.

The GIAs and HAAs are interesting as an area-based approach to housing policy, and they have had a major effect in stimulating 'gentrification' of parts of the inner city. However, their effectiveness in helping those with the greatest housing need was questionable. Balchin (1979) and Babbage (1973) are among those who have argued that the result was that landlords in deprived inner city areas put pressure on poor tenants to vacate their homes, so that higher rents could be charged to a different class of tenant occupying the renovated properties. Furthermore, the scheme was becoming too expensive in the view of the government; in 1983/4 £650 million were spent on improvement grants. In 1984 the government restricted the general availability of 90 per cent grants (Balchin 1985:89).

Meanwhile the problem of poor housing remains a serious one, as shown by the numbers of homes unfit, needing repair or lacking basic amenities, and a recent DoE report (1985) estimated that £19 billion needed to be spent to bring public housing up to standard. Generally the legacy of the high-rise and deck-access constructions of the 1950s and 1960s is now viewed as regrettable. The social effects of the physical fabric of municipal architecture are graphically described by Harrison (1985) and White (1980); and Coleman (1985) has compiled a 'design disadvantagement' score to summarize these undesirable features. The current fashion for 'community architecture', supported by social geographers such as Coleman, is for construction which will preserve the more individual aspects of housing, particularly a sense of territory and personal responsibility for the living space.

Those authorities with large numbers of tower blocks now face the costly problem of rehabilitation or demolition. For example, in Newham, east London, the council decided in 1984 that the remaining blocks in the Ronan Point group showed similar design faults to the block which collapsed in 1968 (Griffiths 1968) and that 580 families would need to be rehoused to allow demolition of the remaining blocks (*Observer*, 13 October 1984). In 1985, in neighbouring Hackney, the failed demolition of a block on the Trowbridge estate drew embarrassing attention to the problems of implementing that authority's policy to demolish all high-rise blocks in the borough. The scale of the housing shortage and of substandard housing means that local authorities in Britain's inner city areas have the heaviest burden in respect of the total financial implications, although it should not be forgotten that in many rural authorities housing provision for local people is also inadequate (Clarke 1982).

The amount which local authorities spend on improving or adding to the local housing stock depends partly on local need and local policies, but also on central government policies. The 1987 White Paper on housing proposed that the private sector should become more involved in rehabilitation of some of the most intractable areas of poorer-standard local authority housing. In 1980, the Local Government, Planning and Land Act established Urban Development Corporations to facilitate this process. One of the best known of these, the London Docklands Development Corporation (LDDC), has certainly generated a considerable amount of private housing construction by making sites available at prices below the true value. However, most of the new units are for owner occupation and are selling at prices considerably above those that the existing population in council housing would be able to pay.

Now the government proposes to extend this policy by developing Housing Action Trusts (HATs), to encourage further injection of private funds into housing development in decaying inner city areas. Ann Power (1988) argues that local authority housing departments have become inflexibly bureaucratic and that new models of housing management should be explored. A similar message was conveyed in the Audit Commission report on the Management of London Authorities (Audit Commission 1987b). According to Power (1988: 50), HATs have potential as catalysts to stimulate action in some of the most problematic estates in Britain's urban areas, 'driving these areas into avant-garde models of city renewal'. However,unless this private investment can be brought to bear on the problem of providing housing for lower-income families who currently live on deprived estates, it seems likely that the HATs will become , in Power's words, 'yet another tale of easy gentrification with government money' (p.50). Local authorities may be left once more to cope with the housing needs of those with the poorest housing status.

Council house sales: residualization of council tenancy

The Housing Act 1980 gave tenants the right to buy their council homes, with discounts according to length of tenure. In the period 1979–83 633,000 homes were sold, which considerably exceeds the number of sales for the whole period 1945–79 (Bryne and Padfield 1985: 255). The response of local authorities to the legislation varied, largely in relation to the political persuasion of the elected council. In 1981, twenty-seven authorities were censured by the government for failing to co-operate, and some such as Sheffield, Stoke, Dagenham, and Greenwich were issued warnings by the Department of the Environment. In Norwich the DoE had to send in agents to ensure compliance with the legislation (Balchin 1985). The rate of council house sales in 1981/2 varied regionally from less than 1 per cent of stock in Greater London to more than 3 per cent in the south-west, the East Midlands, and Wales (Figure 3.5) (Forrest and Murie 1988).

The arguments in favour of the policy of sales were that rented council housing was too expensive to provide in areas like London, and profits for local authorities could be made from the sales. It was also argued that it was not in tenants' interests to remain as tenants, but that they would benefit financially and in terms of security of tenure and independence through becoming owner occupiers. It was thought that the sales might preserve communities by increasing residential stability, and would ease the pressure on the housing market.

The counter-arguments against council house sales questioned the financial benefit to councils over the long term, and suggested that tax relief on mortgages for council homes would also be a financial drain on public resources at the central level. Another serious problem, according to some observers, was that only the more wealthy tenants would be able to buy and only the more desirable homes would be purchased. This may partly explain why, although over a quarter of council homes are flats, these comprised in 1980 only about 2 per cent of council house sales. (However, another reason for the slow rate of sale of council flats is the difficulty of working out satisfactory arrangements with respect to service charges.)

The net result would be a residualization of the council rented sector, which would increasingly be composed of the poorest people, least able to pay rents or mortgages, and occupying the poorest standard accommodation which nobody would want to buy. Balchin (1985) offers some evidence for this residualization on the basis of the tenure characteristics of supplementary benefit (SB) recipients (those whose incomes are so low that they qualify for supplementary payments). In 1972, 55 per cent of recipients were in council tenure, but by 1981 the proportion was 61 per cent. The proportion of council tenants among one-parent families on supplementary benefit had increased from 63 to 76 per cent. However, it should be noted that there had also been some increase in owner occupation amongst SB recipients, and that it was in the privately rented sector that their numbers showed a relative decline.

59

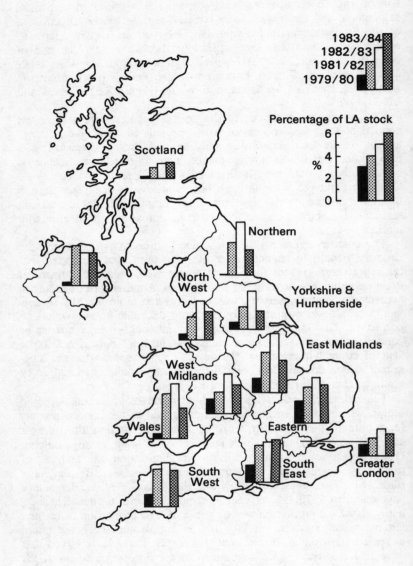

Figure 3.5 Regional distribution of council house sales in the UK: 1980–4.
(Source: Central Statistical Office, *Regional Trends*, 1984, Figure 38.)

Allocation of council homes to rent, and rent control

The main provision of council housing is through the supply of housing to rent, although as we have seen, this role is becoming increasingly limited under the present government policies, leaving the council rented sector increasingly as a 'residual tenure'. In 1981 about one-third of the population in the UK were living in homes rented from local authorities, but as is shown in Table 1.9(p.19), the proportion varies considerably between different parts of the country. The quality of this housing also varies, and access to council tenancies depends on the system of housing allocation. Since demand exceeds supply, the allocation operates through a waiting-list system; over 1 million people were on local authority waiting-lists in 1983 (Association of District Councils *et al.* 1986: 3).

The type of housing likely to be allocated typically depends on need, and on local authority assessment of needs, for example, a typical method of assessment operates on a points system with points allocated according to time waited, family type, standard of present accommodation, domestic standards of the household, and medical needs. Those, such as the homeless, with the most urgent needs are disadvantaged because they may be forced to accept an early offer of accommodation of an inferior standard. Studies of the social profile and previous housing of tenants on council estates have shown that they are socially segregated and that the less attractive estates include a relatively large proportion of less privileged tenants, and of previously homeless people (English 1979; Twine and Williams 1983). The question of access to local authority housing is considered in more detail in Chapter 6, where we shall discuss the position of ethnic minorities in this respect.

Local authority activity in rent control and rebate schemes also has implications for the cost of housing subsidies to local people. The operation of the Housing Benefit Scheme (GB. Parliament 1985a) is a good example of the variable effects on local authorities of providing services to help meet housing needs; the scheme was introduced under the Social Security and Housing Benefits Act 1982, and came into effect in 1983. Local authorities were given new responsibilities for administering housing benefits. The previous scheme had involved the Department of Health and Social Security and local authorities in a dual system of supplementary benefit payments and rent rebates.

There were numerous cases of hardship due to administrative delays as the new scheme came into operation, and it was subject to a review soon afterwards. Kemp (1984) reported on a national survey data for fifty-two local authorities showing that there were variations in the cost to the authorities of administering the scheme, under which supplementary benefit recipients receive a rent rebate in lieu of SB rent and rate allowances. The costs were higher on average in London (£29 per recipient) than elsewhere (where the average cost was £13–£14).

Public transport provided by local authorities

Transportation affects the spatial mobility of populations, their spatial behaviour and preferences for alternative facility locations. This, in turn, affects the catchment areas of facilities such as the schools, hospitals, clinics, and social services centres which form part of welfare provision. These effects are especially important in rural areas (Moseley 1979). Private transport is not universally available, and indeed if it were so, the social and environmental costs would probably be prohibitive. Therefore, for reasons of equity and economy, public provision of communal transport is desirable. Local authority involvement in public transport is mainly in respect of road passenger services. Discussion in this book focuses on bus services and is not concerned with other aspects of transport provision, nor does it consider the responsibility which all local authorities have for maintenance of the road system.

Table 3.3 shows the local authority agencies and national companies responsible for transport provision until 1984. In the GLC and metropolitan counties, Transport Executives provided bus services, accounting for a half of all bus journeys made nationally in 1984. There were also forty-nine councils involved in municipal undertakings, carrying 6 per cent of journeys. These were mainly local services. At the same time, inter-city routes were covered by the National Bus Company (NBC) and the Scottish Bus Group (SBG). Private companies also provided a number of bus services, totalling 30,000 buses and carrying one-third of all journeys in 1984.

Table 3.3 shows that the Transport Executives in the conurbations were the most heavily dependent on subsidies and grants, while private companies received comparatively little in state subsidies. The system of transport grants had developed since 1968, when the Transport Act empowered local authorities to provide funds to subsidize otherwise uneconomic routes. In 1974 a system was introduced whereby local authorities submitted a Transport Policy and Programme Proposal annually to the Department of Transport (DoT). The DoT subsidized agreed proposals to about 60–70 per cent of the total costs.

In 1978 grants were made more widely available to public transport operators, and a consultative document on transport policy declared that 'people have the right to expect a reasonable degree of mobility and the social objective of transport policy is to ensure that this is

Table 3.3   Local authority and national agencies with
responsibility for bus services, and their sources of
income: 1983

| | *Transport agencies* | | | |
	London Transport Executive	*Metropolitan Passenger Transport Executive*	*NBC/ SBG*	*Municipal operators*
%age income from farebox	46	55	76	65
Concessionary fare subsidies	11	13	7	14
Revenue support (grants)	44	32	17	21
Total amount of subsidies 1982/3 (£ million)	272	286	225	48
No. of buses in 1984	5,600	9,600	17,700	5,300

Source: Great Britain, Parliament, 1984.

available' (DoT 1978, p.12). This was to be achieved by a basic
transport network, although what constituted a 'reasonable' degree of
mobility was not defined. Subsidies would be justified, according to
the consultative document, in the case of vulnerable groups such as
elderly, blind, disabled passengers, or the poor, and also to maintain
an adequate service, to avoid excessive fare increases, or to support
innovations in new types of services.

However, when the Conservative government came into power in
1979, there was a change of emphasis (Farrington 1985). The 1980
Transport Act was designed to alter licensing restrictions, especially
for long-haul coach services. The outcomes of the resulting
competition between bus services included an increase in the number
and quality of services on the main inter-city bus routes, and a
reduction of fares. On the other hand, there was an accompanying
reduction of services to intermediate stops and on secondary routes
(Dean 1983).

These outcomes were seen as generally successful by the
government, and the 1984 White Paper on buses (GB. Parliament
1984), embodied in legislation in 1985, brought in more far-reaching
changes. All bus services would be subject to competition, except in

the London area (a separate Act relating to London Transport was passed in 1984). Local authorities have the duty to secure efficient transport which they consider necessary, which does not result from the operation of the free market. To this end, they may invite operators to tender for subsidized services. Transport services were therefore one of the first types of local authority activity which have become subject to competitive tendering under government policies favouring a stronger role for the free market.

The metropolitan Transport Executives were to be broken down into smaller units and become companies which might compete with independent operators to run commercial and subsidized services. Local authorities may also operate concessionary fare schemes. Transitional and innovation grants will be available for rural services, but local authorities will be able to claim Transport Supplementary Grants only with respect to road maintenance, not for provision of bus services.

Thus the role of local authorities has been reduced to one of gap-filling in an essentially market-led bus service industry. The local authorities will no longer have the opportunity to cross-subsidize unprofitable bus routes by more profitable ones, and there is considerable uncertainty over the extent to which subsidized services will be necessary, and the savings which local authorities will be able to make. Two reports prepared by Hertfordshire and Plymouth councils suggest that due to loss of the cross-subsidy, and the need to provide essential services such as extra school bus, social service transport, and works buses, the savings would disappear (*Guardian* 3 December 1984). Glaister (1985) showed that, in London, reduction of subsidies and deregulation would produce smaller, faster, more frequent buses, with higher fares. It therefore seems unlikely that the results of privatization and deregulation will be beneficial for those needing to use the more remote, less commercial routes, especially for those with limited means to pay fares (who might previously have enjoyed fare concessions). However, on the more commercial routes, except in larger urban areas, there is some evidence that services may be improved for the passenger due to pressure of competition.

Welfare administration: the geographical perspective

The preceding chapters have shown two important geographical dimensions of welfare administration. First, the division of the national space into administrative areas for the purposes of welfare provision has implications for the organization and operation of the service, and determines geographical variations in patterns of provision between

(¹)

areas. Second, the relationship between central government and local *(ii)* government is a complex one with respect to welfare provision, and has profound effects on the response of authorities to welfare needs. A growth in centralized control is recognizable, and will be discussed in more detail in Chapter 7.

In the 1980s we have seen a clear trend towards the reduction of the role of the public sector in Britain, especially of local government with respect to welfare provision. Parallel developments are a growth in the activity of the private, voluntary, and informal sectors. The introduction of free market competition is likely to have a profound effect on the way that services are provided; and we have already discussed competitive tendering for public transport provision. Other services which are to be subject to competitive tendering include school and welfare catering and cleansing of public places. The implications of these trends for the geography of welfare provision to particular client groups are discussed in the following chapters.

Political and ideological differences, and differences in the philosophy of care between authorities, as well as division of responsibilities for welfare services within jurisdictional areas, are all factors which influence the ways that clients' needs are defined and how services attempt to meet these needs. For health and social care, there has been a trend towards national and local policies to integrate services to provide a holistic and well-co-ordinated package of care to particular types of client. However, major administrative and operational divisions still persist between different welfare service functions. Medical and social provision have separate administrations, and housing and education are provided by separate departments of local authorities. Vulnerable groups, such as children, old people, and ethnic minorities, may need to resort to several different agencies providing for their welfare needs. The following chapters consider how the system operates for these client groups.

Chapter four

Young children and their families

The social geography of children in the UK

The geography of need for children's welfare services is affected by the spatial distribution of the child population and by the geographical experience of young people. In the UK young people acquire most adult rights, such as voting, at the age of 18, but it is the population under the age of 16 who comprise the principal client group for most of the services considered here. Children are at their most vulnerable in their early years, and much of the discussion in this chapter relates to the youngest age-groups, especially the under-5s.

The Census of population provides information on the distribution of children in the UK space. In 1981, 12.1 million children under 16 years were enumerated in Britain (22 per cent of the total population). Children under 5 years comprised 3.2 million (6 per cent). The child population is particularly concentrated in suburban areas of the country, especially in areas such as the Midlands, Merseyside, and the Home Counties, and in parts of Scotland (Figure 4.1). The highest proportions of children in the population are found in the new towns of Cumbernauld, Milton Keynes and Tamworth (over 28 per cent). Children represent a relatively low proportion of the population in the inner city, especially in London (only 13 per cent of the population of Westminster, Kensington, and Chelsea were under 16). In retirement areas, especially coastal resorts where elderly people are numerous, children also form a relatively small proportion of the population.

The relative size of the child population varies quite markedly over time, as well as space, due to fluctuations in the birth rate. Over the inter-censal period 1961–71 the number in the under-16 age-group increased by 9 per cent, but it declined by 12 per cent during 1971–81, and is expected to have fallen a further 6 per cent by 1991. The number of children under 5 also fell during 1971-81 by 26 per cent, but since the birth rate rose in the 1980s, the population under 5 is projected to increase by 22.6 per cent between 1981 and 1991. Such

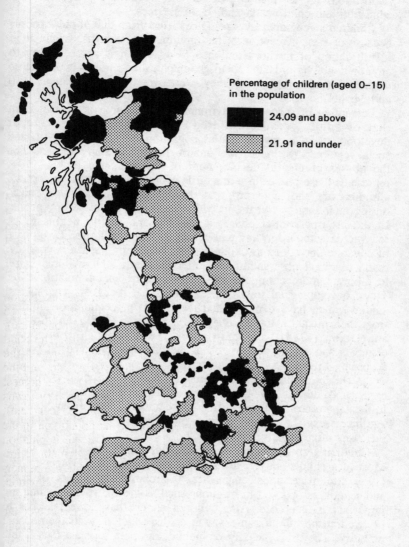

Percentage of children (aged 0–15)
in the population

■ 24.09 and above

▨ 21.91 and under

Figure 4.1 The child population of Britain: 1981. (Source: OPCS, 1984b.)

67

fluctuations in the size of different age-groups has important implications for the planning of services for children, especially for education and child health and social services.

Children's geographical experience differs from that of older people because of their perception of the environment, their behaviour, their identification of territory and use of space, their susceptibility to environmental hazards, the socio-geographical constraints operating on them, and the control which they exert over their environment (Hill and Michelson 1981).

Perception of space and environment by children is distinct from that of adults because children are at an immature stage of development in terms of spatial cognition, physical capacity, and social relationships. Piaget was one of the first to study and describe the phases of mental development in children, and Piche (1981) represents these phases in terms of development of spatial perception. Children are shown to progress through the sensori-motor phase, during their first two years, in which the world is defined by action. In the pre-operational phase, up to 7 years, reality begins to be interpreted without forming real concepts. This is followed by a phase of concrete operations as children begin to interpret space beyond the realm of direct observation, and after the age of 11, children begin to elborate more complex, adult concepts of spatial relationships. These developmental trends have formed the focus of geographical studies which have demonstrated the spatial perceptions of children from their mental maps. Matthews (1981), Piche (1981), and Spencer and Dixon (1983) have shown, for example, that the important elements and spatial dimensions of the city are perceived differently according to the age of the subject.

As children grow older, their area of activity and spatial knowledge expands. Matthews (1984) has shown that the general trend is for the furthest point correctly identified to be more distant from home as age increases. The rate of increase of the sphere of spatial cognition increases more rapidly with age.

Children's spatial behaviour is also different from that of adults. Most of a child's activity involves education and play. Hagerstrand's (1969) life space model emphasizes the relative importance of home and school, as opposed to locations such as the workplace, which are important in later life. Also children do not have direct access to private transport in the same way as adults, which restricts their spatial mobility. They rely heavily on public transport services (see Table 4.1), especially since women who are most often concerned with child care also have less access to private transport than do men (see Chapter 5).

Table 4.1 Bus travel, by age-group, in Britain: 1978/9

Sex	Age-group (years)	Number stage bus journeys/person/week
Males and females	0–4	1.3
	5–10	1.1
	11–15	3.2
Males	16–20	3.9
	21–29	2.2
	30–59	1.5
	60–64	2.3
	65+	2.5
Females	16–20	5.6
	21–29	2.6
	30–59	2.7
	60–64	3.2
	65+	2.8
All individuals		2.4

Source: Great Britain, Parliament, 1984, table 11.

All these aspects of the geographical experience of children mean that they are strongly affected by conditions within their immediate environment. The elements of the environment which are useful and valuable for children (play space, educational facilities, and opportunities for safe exploration of an expanding action space) are dissimilar to, and may be incompatible with, those of adults.

Factors relating to children's welfare needs

Children seem particularly susceptible to detrimental social or physical environments, which may have long-term effects on their life chances. The idea of the cycle of disadvantage was first introduced to the discussion of social deprivation in childhood by Keith Joseph speaking as Secretary of State for Education in 1972, who commented that: 'perhaps there is at work here a process...by which problems reproduce themselves from generation to generation' (Robinson 1976: 32).

Several studies, including those discussed in Chapter 1, have observed the transmission of poverty between generations (e.g. Atkinson, Maynard, and Trinder 1983; Wedge and Prosser 1973). The link between childhood poverty and poor educational achievement, and subsequent poorer life chances, has been demonstrated by several cohort studies of British children (Douglas and Bloomfield 1958; Davie, Butler, and Goldstein 1972; Osborne *et al.*, 1984).

Generalizations about the factors related to childhood deprivation may be misleading if rigidly extrapolated to individual families, but in aggregate, conditions of family stress do seem to be associated with lower levels of well-being among children. Groups of children who are relatively likely to suffer socio-economic disadvantage include those whose parents belong to less privileged occupational groups, or those in families where the wage-earner is unemployed. While the proportion of children in the semi- and unskilled occupational groups has declined slightly over recent years, the proportion of parents who are unemployed has increased quite considerably over the period 1979–84 (Tables 4.2 and 4.3). Unemployment among both mothers and fathers has risen, and probably by more than the published figures suggest, since unemployed women are often not registered as looking for work. As this results in economic difficulty in families, the effects are detrimental to children, and results in a greater need for support services. This must be weighed against the child care needs of mothers in paid work, which will also have implications for local authorities in terms of need for services, as discussed below.

Another group which has caused considerable concern is that with an atypical family pattern (i.e. not the conventional family of husband, wife, and dependent children). The majority of children live in families including a married couple, but in 1981, 13 per cent lived in other types of family, and about 6 per cent were living in one-parent families. This group is important because it is relatively deprived economically, and tends to have greater needs for publicly provided services and facilities. Lone-parent families often face particular socio-economic difficulties. Evidence of this was systematically presented at the national scale in the Finer Report (GB. Parliament 1974). More recent data for 1981, shown in Table 4.4, indicates that one-parent households have lower average disposable incomes, are more likely to lack basic amenities in their housing, and are more likely to live in council housing and less likely to dwell in owner occupation than families with two parents.

The health of children is one aspect of well-being which is related to social environment. Blaxter (1981) has reviewed the evidence for links between socio-economic disadvantage and health of children. Young people are also particularly affected by physical environmental hazards in the home and outside, such as risk of accidents (MacFarlane and Fox 1978; Jackson 1986) and polluted or damp atmospheric conditions (Blaxter 1981: 106; Douglas and Waller 1966; Hunt, Martin, and Platt 1986).

Table 4.2 Characteristics of the child population: 1979–84

	Children surveyed in the General Household Survey			
	1979		1984	
	(no.)	*(%)*	*(no.)*	*(%)*
Children aged 0–15 *by occupational group* *of household*				
Professional	478	6.5	330	5.9
Employers and managers	1,255	17.3	1,090	19.6
Intermediate and junior non-manual	1,154	15.9	952	17.1
Skilled manual and own-account non-professional	2,864	39.4	2,093	37.7
Semi-skilled manual and personal service	1,208	16.6	878	15.8
Unskilled manual	305	4.2	211	3.8
Total	7,264		5,554	
Dependent children, *by type of family**				
Married couple		88		88
Lone mother		10		11
Lone father		1		1

* GHS, 1984, table 3.8, p. 13; dependent children include those under 16 or aged 16–18 in full-time education and living in the household; percentages have been rounded to the nearest whole % figure.
Source: OPCS. 1986a

Table 4.3 Economic activity of married people of working age with dependent children

	Employment status of General Household Survey sample			
	1979		1984	
	(%age *working)*	*(%age* *unemployed)*	*(%age* *working)*	*(%age* *unemployed)*
Survey respondents *responsible for children*				
Married men with dependent children	94	4	87	10
Married women with dependent children	60	2	57	4
Lone mothers	47*		39*	

* Information for lone mothers does not include data on those unemployed; the figure for 1979 is derived from combined data for 1978–80, and the 1984 figure is from data for 1982–84.
Source: OPCS, 1986a, tables 6.6 and 6.7.

Table 4.4   Socio-economic attributes of one-parent and
two-parent families

Attribute	One-parent families	Two-parent families
Average disposable income 1981 (£)	96.83	156.28
%age households lacking a bath	0.7	1.2
%age households lacking a WC	1.4	2.0
%age households with a car	29	81
%age living in council rented homes	59	27
%age living in owner occupied homes	36	65

Source: OPCS, 1984b, 1987.

Children therefore have special needs to ensure normal emotional, intellectual, and physical growth (Bowlby 1956; Kelmer Pringle 1975). They require conditions which will meet their basic physical needs, and needs for satisfactory personal relations with adults, for suitable identifications and feelings of security and self-worth. They need to learn to cope with impulses and develop self-discipline and socially acceptable behaviour, to make choices, distinguish between right and wrong, and to communicate (Advisory Council on Child Care 1974).

Welfare services are intended to support, supplement, or substitute parental care in providing for these needs of children. Local authorities have responsibilities to provide services for education and careers advice, care and protection of deprived children, day care of pre-school children, and care of young handicapped people. Since the geographical and environmental experience of young people differs from other groups in the population, their needs for welfare services and facilities are also distinct, and it will be necessary to resolve competing demands for resources between the child clients of the welfare services and those of older users.

In the UK the social indicators associated with risks to children, and with greater need for children's services, are unevenly distributed in space, and tend to be greater in the north of the country compared with the south and west, with particularly high concentrations in the inner cities. The regional distribution of income and unemployment levels in the UK space were considered in Chapter 1, and Table 4.5 shows the varying proportion of one-parent families and working mothers. Birth rates and perinatal mortality rates also shown in the table indicate the parts of the country where the number of pre-school children are likely to be growing most rapidly, and those areas where child health seems to be most at risk in the early years.

Local authorities in areas such as deprived inner cities must therefore make provision for the higher relative needs of their child populations, although the absolute numbers of children are typically smaller than in other parts of the UK. The following sections consider the implications for education, health, and social services to young people.

Area-based policies for education

One response to the problem of the cycle of deprivation has been through schemes for positive discrimination through the education system, which have a strong geographical dimension. In 1967 the Plowden Report (Central Advisory Council for Education 1967) recommended positive discrimination in favour of children seen to have particular educational difficulty, and defined Educational Priority Areas (EPAs) in terms of a set of area social indicators, shown in Table 4.6. In these areas schools should receive additional resources beyond those necessary to achieve equalization of standards, in order to compensate children for deprivation. The report also emphasized nursery education and pre-school care as a means of intervention to alleviate the effects of deprivation. In 1967 the government allocated £16 million for educational improvement in areas of multiple deprivation. This was spent on buildings and teachers' salaries in schools of exceptional social difficulty. By the end of 1968, 572 primary schools (2.5 per cent of all LEA schools) received some finance for these purposes.

The expansion of nursery education was a favoured policy in the 1970s when the falling birth rate was causing a decline in primary school rolls. In 1972 a further commitment was made to development of nursery education in the policy document entitled *Education: A Framework for Expansion* (DES 1972), which proposed that nursery education should be provided on demand for 3- and 4-year-olds, resulting in an estimated 75 per cent of 4-year-olds and 35 per cent of 3-year-olds receiving such education.

The Urban Programme has also contributed to EPA schemes. The original Urban Aid Programme, established under the Local Government Grants (Social Need) Act 1969, applied to all local authorities with large populations affected by poor physical

Table 4.5 Regional variations in selected indicators relating to need for child care services

Region (metropolitan area)	Percentage of children in 1981		Live births per 1,000 population 1985	Perinatal mortality rate, 1983–5*	Infant mortality rate, 1985*
	Living with one adult only	With mother working full time			
North	6.0	12.5	13.2	10.5	9.8
(Tyne and Wear)	7.0	12.1	12.6	11.2	
Yorkshire and Humberside	5.9	12.2	13.2	11.1	10.6
(South Yorkshire)	5.4	11.8	12.7	10.5	
(West Yorkshire)	6.6	14.1	14.0	11.4	
East Midlands	5.4	13.5	12.9	9.8	8.9
East Anglia	5.1	11.0	12.5	9.3	9.8
South-east	6.5	13.5	13.2	9.3	9.2
(Greater London)	8.6	16.5	14.3	9.6	
South-west	5.6	10.7	11.9	9.2	9.1
West Midlands	5.7	13.7	13.6	12.1	11.7
(West Midlands)	6.5	13.6	14.4	12.5	
North-west	6.5	15.4	13.8	10.1	10.0
(Greater Manchester)	6.9	16.7	14.3	10.2	
(Merseyside)	7.0	11.7	13.9	9.4	
England	6.1	13.2	13.1	10.0	9.8
Wales	5.7	13.7	13.1	10.7	10.2
Scotland	6.1	14.5	13.0	10.5	9.8
Northern Ireland	4.8	26.3	17.7	11.6	11.1

Table 4.6   Indicators for educational priority areas recommended by the Plowden Report

---

EPAs would be defined as those with high proportions of children with:

(a)   parents in unskilled/semi-skilled occupations;

(b)   large families;

(c)   families receiving welfare benefits;

(d)   families living in overcrowded/shared dwellings;

(e)   poor records for attendance/truancy at school;

(f)   problems of educational retardation, disturbed behaviour, handicap;

(g)   incomplete families;

(h)   poor ability to speak English

Source: Central Advisory Council for Education, 1967.

environment and housing standards, large families, persistent unemployment, or children in trouble or in care of the local authority. After 1977, the Urban Aid Programme was recast, with priority for Inner City Partnerships in Newcastle, Manchester, Liverpool, Birmingham, Lambeth, Islington/Hackney, and the Docklands area of inner London. Other authorities included in the revised Urban Programme were Tyneside, Sunderland, Middlesbrough, Bolton, Oldham, Wirral, Bradford, Hull, Leeds, Sheffield, Leicester, Nottingham, Wolverhampton, and Hammersmith. Higgins *et al.* (1983:69–72) have shown that of the various projects supported, those for nursery education have received the largest single share of funds under the Urban Programme (12.2 per cent) and a further 12.7 per cent went to pre-school playgroups, day nurseries and day care.

The EPA approach illustrates the problems of area-based programmes of positive discrimination. Several studies have examined the effectiveness of EPA policies, and have questioned how well the characteristics of individuals can be predicted from the attributes of the neighbourhood where they live (the problem referred to in geography as the 'ecological fallacy'). We may also ask whether conditions for those most in need can be improved by putting resources into community facilities (Robinson 1976; Gray 1978; Jones and Eyles 1977; Williams and Bryne 1979).

The Educational Priority Area (EPA) project during the 1970s (Halsey 1972) investigated the potential of education as an effective means of positive discrimination. This was an action research project based in areas of exceptional social difficulty (Balsall Heath, Birmingham; Liverpool; Deptford, London; and Denaby, Doncaster, with a parallel study carried out in Dundee). The main form of intervention was by means of pre-school education, and the objectives were to raise educational performance of children, to raise morale of teachers, to increase involvement of parents, and the sense of responsiblity for community among local residents. It demonstrated the significance of factors outside, as well as within, school experience in determining educational disadvantage, and the evidence of improved achievement was equivocal. However, Halsey recommended retention of the social priority area as a focus for positive discrimination, and continuation of locally based intervention to encourage parental involvement and improve links between home and school. Halsey's report advocated nursery education as of benefit to children and parents, although he has also commented that educational opportunity is not likely to affect life chances without corresponding employment chances for school-leavers (Halsey 1972; Halsey 1980).

The EPA approach has been criticized for failing to direct resources effectively towards a significant proportion of those in need. For example, Barnes and Lucas (1974) found that EPA schools taught 13.6 per cent of all children but only 20.2 per cent of the disadvantaged. Compared with EPAs, other parts of the country outside the priority areas contained five times as many children in large families, five times the number of children of unskilled workers, 4.5 times as many with low verbal and reasoning scores and 3.5 the number receiving free school meals.

Cullingford and Openshaw (1979) showed from the National Child Development Study data that the relation between area and individual data was most variable in the inner city. Information from the Survey of Child Health and Education in the 1970s was used to compile indices of disadvantage both for children and the neighbourhoods where they lived. However, 59 per cent of the most disadvantaged were outside the poorest neighbourhoods.

On the other hand, there is some evidence which argues for an EPA approach. Robson (1969) found that in Sunderland there was more variation in intelligence quotient(IQ) ratings of pupils between classes than between areas, but that in some areas children had particularly low average IQ. He commented on the conflict facing more successful working-class pupils who had to leave their local area to attend grammar schools in more middle-class areas. Little and Mabey (1973) found that the character of the school was a less powerful predictor of achievement than the type of area from which a pupil came, and the authors advocate the retention of EPAs. Williamson and Bryne

(1979) also conclude that although there are fundamental structural explanations for the cycle of deprivation, which imply more far-reaching socio-political action, a geographical approach to social intervention through the education system is relevant because of the spatial organized and spatially differentiated nature of the education system in this country. They argue that, 'schools have catchment areas ... and these can become barriers which divide children along social class lines' (p. 197).

Furthermore, since attitudes within schools and communities are apparently so important to pupils' chances, it is probably necessary to try to introduce higher standards and promote morale in schools in areas where levels of deprivation are worst, otherwise the education system will tend to exacerbate the existing social disadvantages. The problem of school provision to deprived communities is given further consideration in Chapter 6, where we shall consider the position of children from ethnic minorities. The geographical concentration of EPAs, especially in Britain's inner cities, contributes towards the varying patterns of educational and welfare provision to children and families, and the differences in the unit costs of education. The spatial patterns of service provision are considered in the following sections.

The geography of pre-school provision

Local authorities are involved to a varying degree in sharing with parents the care of children under 5 years. The *General Household Survey* of 1979 (OPCS 1980b) showed that about half of all under-5s in Britain received day care outside the home. The provision made takes the form of several types of service, which differ in the objectives and nature of the care they provide.

Nursery education, in nursery or first-year primary classes, is intended to provide education to supplement home experience, as well as physical care of children, and normally provides care for part or all of the school day, but not throughout the entire period of adult working hours. The DES statistics for the UK in 1987 indicated that there were about 176 places per 1,000 chidren under 5, and 44 per cent of children under 5 years received nursery education.

Playgroups have a different philosophy of care, being intended to provide education through play. They are largely voluntary, although they may be supported by local authorities, and they usually only provide part-day sessions. These are not services intended primarily for children of working parents, since they often require involvement on the part of parents. Because experience in schools or playgroups helps to promote the intellectual development of young children, these are the types of pre-school care which parents prefer (Bone 1978).

77

About 476,100 places were available for children in playgroups in 1987 (approx. 13 per cent of the total number of children under 5).

Day nurseries provide a service with emphasis on physical care for children, as a substitute for parental care when parents are working or are otherwise unable to provide suitable home care. They may also provide educational experience for children. Day nurseries are often available for longer hours than schools, since they are providing a support service to working parents as well as children, and those provided by social service departments are often seen as a preventative service, to avoid admission into care for high-risk children who are handicapped or are from socially deprived or one-parent families. The number of local authority day nursery places is limited; in 1987 there were about 59,500 places in the UK (16 per 1,000 under-5s on average).

Finally, childminders provide a substitute for parental care in a domestic setting which may be very satisfactory for children of working parents. However, the standard of care is very variable. Childminders are required to be registered and inspected by local authorities, but many provide informal services without registration which are well below acceptable standards. It is difficult to estimate the number of children receiving care from childminders. The *General Household Survey* for 1979 indicated that 1 per cent of under-5s in the sample were looked after by childminders, but another 2 per cent were cared for by a neighbour or friend and 6 per cent by a relative outside the household. The DHSS figures for 1987 indicated 144,000 registered places with childminders in the UK, about 40 per 1,000 of the population under 5. However, there are likely to be many more unregistered places.

Table 4.7 shows the variable level of provision for pre-school children in nursery education and day nurseries in different parts of the UK in the mid-1980s. The higher level of provision of day care in urban areas is partly explained by the social needs of children in urban areas and EPAs already discussed, but analysis of the spending by social service departments on child care services have shown that expenditure on under-5s is not entirely determined by varying social need and may also result from varying policies of local authorities (Bebbington and Curtis 1981). The geographical variations have considerable implications in terms of access to the benefits of pre-school day care, which affect not only children's opportunities for social and intellectual growth, but their parents' opportunities to take paid employment and to be supported in the task of child care by the welfare state.

Table 4.7 Levels of provision of education and day care for under-5s, by region: 1984/5

Region	Numbers of places (000s) in:				Places/100 under-5s in:	
	Maintained schools	Day nursery	Sessional playgroups	Childminders	Schools	Other day care
North	52.8	2.4	21.0	4.8	27	14
Yorkshire and Humberside	69.5	4.2	33.4	8.8	22	15
East Midlands	41.4	3.1	33.1	9.4	17	19
East Anglia	16.3	1.3	21.2	5.6	14	23
South-east	143.2	24.4	161.3	56.9	13	23
South-west	32.0	2.2	46.8	10.6	12	23
West Midlands	67.1	5.6	15.6	42.1	20	19
North-west	90.3	10.6	44.0	15.3	22	17
England	512.6	53.8	402.7	53.8	20	17
Wales	50.3	1.2	19.7	4.2	28	14
Scotland	48.2	4.1	43.9	7.5	15	17
Northern Ireland	25.5	0.3	9.8	5.0	19	11
UK	636.6	59.5	476.1	143.5	18	19

Source: Central Statistical Office, Regional Trends, 1987.

The geography of child health and welfare services

In addition to education and day care services, welfare provision for children includes health care such as maternity services, child health surveillance, and immunization which are normally carried out by health authorities. The Court Report (GB. Parliament 1976a) examined the need to develop child health care, especially for disadvantaged groups, for whom the uptake of health care is relatively low, in spite of their poorer average health experience (Blaxter 1981). The report suggested changes including a more integrated system of health care, linking family doctors, paediatricians, and health visitors.

Need for child health care shows some spatial differentiation. The geographical and social dimensions of infant mortality have already been commented on (see Chapter 1). Areas where the birth rate is high are often areas where the perinatal mortality rate is also above average, particularly in metropolitan areas (see Table 4.5). In these parts of the UK improvement of the accessibility of health services for children is of particular concern. Good child health care requires well-integrated primary health services, and as we have already observed (Chapter 3), the co-ordination of community health services is especially problematic in major urban areas.

In some cases, child care services may be required to provide a substitute for parental care which extends beyond sharing day care for children who are deprived of normal home life. In 1982 there were more than 93,000 children 'in care' of local authorities in England and Wales (about 75/10,000 of the population under 18). Of these, approximately 10 per cent were under 5 years of age. Children may come into care because they are placed voluntarily by their parents who are unable to provide for them, or under a 'care order' in cases of child abuse, or moral danger to the child, and when the child is beyond the care or control of the parents. Juvenile offenders may be committed to the care of local authorities under court orders.

Factors associated with risk of admission to care include abnormal family pattern (marital breakdown, illegitimacy, death or illness of parents, or absence or imprisonment of a parent); inadequate parenting (mental or physical incapacity of parents or a difficult relationship between the child and parents); unsatisfactory home environment (poverty, homelessness, detrimental neighbourhood factors); or a child's behavioural problems due to handicap or psychological disturbance (Creighton 1980; Kempe and Kempe 1976; Kelmer Pringle 1975; Lambert and Rowe 1973). There is a positive spatial association between social deprivation and higher proportions of children in care. Although both factors show a good deal of local variation, they tend in general to be above average in the North of

England and Scotland, and in the major metropolitan areas (Tables 4.5 and 4.8). The costs of child care provision are considerable, and have large resource implications for social service departments in local authorities where the admission rate is high.

Generally speaking admission to care is a 'last resort' solution to family problems, and in areas where the admission rate is high, local authorities often deploy significant social service resources on 'preventative' social work and services such as day nurseries to alleviate the risk of admission. It is partly for this reason that day nursery provision is particularly high in some deprived inner city areas. Some local authorities have also tried to stimulate community

Table 4.8   Regional variations in the proportion of children under 18 years in local authority care

Region	Metropolitan area	No. of children in care /1,000 under 18 in 1985
North		6.7
	Tyne and Wear	8.2
Yorkshire and Humberside		6.5
	South Yorkshire	5.8
	West Yorkshire	7.4
East Midlands		6.1
East Anglia		4.7
South-east		6.0
	Greater London	8.3
South-west		4.7
West Midlands		6.2
	West Midlands	7.4
North-west		7.6
	Greater Manchester	8.7
	Merseyside	8.0
England		6.1
Wales		5.5
Scotland		10.6
Northern Ireland		5.0
UK		6.5

Source: As Table 4.7.

action for better child care in socially deprived areas, by initiating playgroups, for example. These initiatives have been criticized as ineffective and hypocritical by some observers (e.g. Finch 1984, Ferri and Niblett 1977). However, there does seem to be general consensus that better co-ordination between health, education, and social services and the voluntary sector are essential to promote good child care practices generally, and to reduce the risk of admission to care in cases of extreme family difficulty.

About half the children received into care are 'boarded out' in foster homes, which provide a substitute for the family environment, and usually are the preferred type of placement because it is considered better for the child's well-being, and because the average cost is lower. Alternatively, children may be cared for in one of a number of different types of residential home.

The proportion of children in care who are boarded out varies between different areas in the UK. It is sometimes argued that local authorities have particular difficulties providing foster home placements when the children in their care have characteristics which make them 'hard to place', or where the supply of foster homes is especially limited. However, Davies, Barton, and McMillan (1971) and Packman (1975) found little relationship between indicators of these factors in local authorities and the 'balance of care' between foster and residential home placements. It seems that local policy and practice is also an influential factor. Chapter 6 considers the foster care needs of children from ethnic minorities who come into care.

Therefore, for children of families under stress, the range of social services available will vary according to their local authority of residence, because of the differing ways in which social service departments respond to local population need and the use made of community resources by the statutory services.

Spatial aspects of supplementary, complementary, and compensatory services to children

This chapter has shown that services to children are considered to be a particularly important element of welfare provision because children are especially susceptible to the impact of their environment, and childhood experience, especially in the early years, may have an influence throughout later life. In British society it is accepted that welfare services have a role to play in complementing and supplementing the care which children normally receive from their parents, by providing health and education and opportunities for experience outside the family home. In addition, the welfare services are required to provide additional inputs for some communities to ompensate children for the detrimental effects of environmental actors which have an uneven spatial as well as social pattern.

As discussed in Chapter 3, local authorities still exercise some utonomy in deciding policies for education and social services, and ccess to such services for families with children will depend on how ocal authorities interpret their responsibilities in this field. The rovision made to children has implications for all households, ncluding those which do not include children. The cost to the ommunity of providing child care, especially in the early years, is onsiderable. Nevertheless, it is in the interests of the community enerally to invest in services which can be so fundamental to hildren's well-being, and may help to shape the contribution which ley may make to society in later life.

Chapter five

Welfare provision for the elderly

The social geography of ageing

Chapter 4 concerned the implications for welfare provision of
differences in the spatial distribution and geographical experience of
children, who are particularly vulnerable to their social and physical
environment and have special needs as clients for welfare
services. This chapter demonstrates that those at the other extreme of
the age spectrum also have characteristics which are important for the
geography of welfare provision.

As people grow older, their geographical experience changes.
Rowles (1980) has postulated 'life-world adjustment' with respect to
action, orientation, feeling, and fantasy. These adjustments often
included a restriction of the daily action space, and more intensive
use of some foci in the locality. However, old age and retirement
might also provide new opportunities for travel or residential
movement over longer distances than during earlier life. These
changes are important for the spatial distribution of the elderly, as
shown below. Elderly people were depicted as becoming orientated
increasingly towards less hazardous and less physically demanding
environments, and towards the home and the immediate residential
locality. Places may be valued for their emotive qualities, and local
community spirit will be highly valued. The residential locality may
be perceived through the filter of reminiscences, while the life world
beyond the action space will also figure in the projective fantasy of
an elderly person. Thus the requirements of elderly people and their
capacity to make use of the opportunities offered by their local area
may differ from younger populations, and this has implications for
their choice of areas of residence and demands for services.

The 1981 Census of population showed that 18 per cent (9.7
million) of the British population was of pensionable age (men over
65 and women over 60). However, this proportion varied widely
between local authorities, from 35 per cent in Rother and Worthing

84

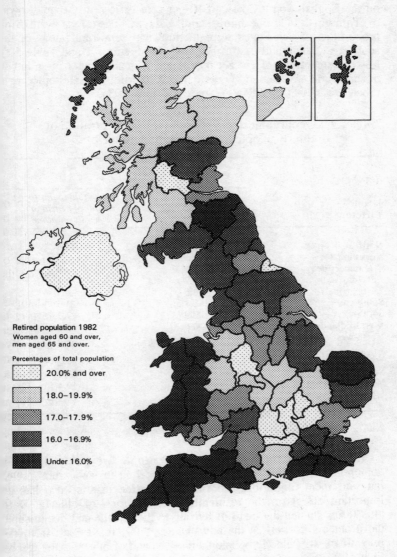

Retired population 1982
Women aged 60 and over,
men aged 65 and over.

Percentages of total population

20.0% and over

18.0–19.9%

17.0–17.9%

16.0–16.9%

Under 16.0%

Figure 5.1 Retired population of the UK: 1982 (percentages of population). (Source: Central Statistical Office, *Regional Trends*, 1982, p. 49.)

on the English South Coast, to 10 per cent or less in the new town
of Tamworth, Cumbernauld, and Kilsyth. The areas with high
proportions of pensioners were in rural and semi-rural areas of the
south-west, south and east of England (see Figure 5.1 and Table 5.1
Lower percentages of elderly people are typically found in suburban
or semi-rural areas around London, the West Midlands, and other main
urban areas (OPCS 1984a; Warnes and Law 1984).

Table 5.1 Geographical variations in the concentration of
elderly people living alone in Britain: 1982

Regions	Percentage of:	
	Population of pensionable age	*Households comprising people of pensionable age living alone*
North	17.5	23.6
Yorkshire and Humberside	18.0	25.0
East Midlands	17.2	23.4
East Anglia	18.8	25.5
South-east	18.1	23.8
South-west	20.9	27.3
West Midlands	16.5	22.0
North-west	17.9	24.5
Wales	18.8	24.2
Scotland	17.0	23.4
Northern Ireland	14.4	19.4
UK	17.9	23.5

Source: Central Statistical Office, *Regional Trends*, 1982, pp. 30–1.

The high concentrations of elderly people are partly due to a
demographic history of senescence and decline in some rural areas
but retirement migration, especially to seaside resorts, also has an
important effect on the residential concentration of elderly. Karn
(1977) has studied the trend of retiring to the seaside and documented
the problems as well as the advantages of this movement, from the
point of view of elderly people themselves and of others in the resort
such as doctors and other welfare providers. Law and Warnes (1982)
in their study of the retirement decision of a sample of elderly people
found that nearly 45 per cent searched for retirement homes in coastal
areas only. Only 8.5 per cent restricted themselves to the area of their
pre-retirement home, the majority preferring to move further afield

The choice of retirement location will be influenced by knowledge and perceptions of the area. Warnes and Law showed that 20 per cent of the elderly people in their sample had not visited their retirement area before moving there, and of those that had, many did so for holidays. The holiday impressions of a place may differ from the reality of full-time residence, and this may account for the fact that not all retirement migrants are happy with their new homes. The pre-existing social contacts in an area may assist integration into a new community, but 40 per cent of the elderly interviewed by Warnes and Law had no previous social contacts in the area they moved to.

In line with the rest of the British population, elderly people have shown a tendency during the last decade to move from inner city areas towards the suburbs of large cities. Thus, for example, the total population of pensioners in inner London fell by 52,000 in the inter-censal period 1971–81, while in outer London the total increased by 37,000 (Ingram 1983). However, counter-urbanization has apparently affected the elderly in the inner city less than younger groups of the urban population, so that relative size of the elderly population in inner London increased from 16.4 to nearly 18 per cent over the same period. Also in resort towns the greatest recent growth of the elderly population has been in the suburbs, although high concentrations remain in the town centres (Warnes and Law 1984).

The elderly are not a homogeneous group, although we can make some generalizations about them compared with younger populations. A distinction must be made, for example, between younger pensioners and the 'old old', over 75 years. The latter group is important for the welfare services, because of their greater frailty and physical and social dependency, and their relatively high rate of need and use of health and social care. This group has increased from 2.3 million in 1961 (30 per cent of pensioners) to 3.1 million in 1981 (32 per cent) and will increase most rapidly over the next two decades according to OPCS predictions (to 41 per cent of pensioners in the year 2001). These elderly people are expected to consume an increasing proportion of welfare service resources in future. Their geographical distribution corresponds to that for the pensionable population generally, and is especially concentrated in the older retirement areas. The relative size of this group has also grown quickly in metropolitan areas over the 1970s (outside the GLC, the increase exceeds 16 per cent). In future years the areas of most rapid growth will be in new retirement areas as the recently retired population ages.

The elderly living alone are also a particularly vulnerable group, totalling 2.8 million in 1981 (31 per cent of the pensionable population). The greatest concentrations of elderly living alone in 1981 were in rural areas in the Pennines and in Scotland and Wales, around the south-east coast of England, in declining industrial areas of north-east England and Lancashire (Table 5.1). There are also high percentages of lone elderly people in some of the inner London boroughs (e.g. Westminster and Tower Hamlets). Thus, in some urban areas, problems of socio-economic deprivation among the younger population occur in combination with high proportions of vulnerable elderly, presenting competing needs for welfare resources in these areas.

Mobility and transport needs of the elderly

The different geographical experience of elderly people has already been commented on in the previous section. The travel patterns of elderly people are evidence of more restricted daily spatial mobility than among the younger population. In Chapter 1 social class differences in travel behaviour have been noted. Information from the 1978–9 National Travel Survey (Table 4.1) also shows that the elderly make fewer, shorter journeys than younger adults. Elderly people, especially women, are particularly likely to use public transport, especially buses. As shown in Table 4.1, only young people under 20 make more frequent bus journeys than pensioners. Car ownership is an important factor detemining dependence on public transport. The 1981 Census showed that 27 per cent of households which included only pensioners had a household car, compared with 61 per cent of all households nationally. Five million elderly people live in households without a car, and among women over the age of 75 and living alone only 5 per cent are car owners.

The real costs of stage bus fares increased by about 30 per cent from 1972 to 1983, and apart from short periods of relative decline in 1972, 1973, and 1978, the trend has been consistently upwards, and at a faster rate than motoring costs, which have been much more stable since 1975 (Figure 5.2). The elderly, who are particularly disadvantaged in terms of ability to pay, are significantly affected by the availability of concessionary fare schemes offered by local bus operators to offset the effects of higher fares. These vary widely from one part of the country to another. In the late 1970s it was reported that fifty non-metropolitan local government districts had no concessionary fares scheme (for example, there were none in Cornwall, and only one in five districts in Wiltshire operated such schemes). It was estimated that of 9 million pensioners in England, 800,000 lived in areas with no concession. Where schemes did operate, the level of concession varied (GB. Parliament 1979c). In contrast, 2.4 million elderly people benefited from free bus travel, mainly in metropolitan areas, while 5 million were in areas with

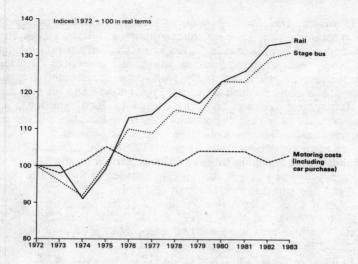

Figure 5.2 Trends in stage bus fares compared with motoring and rail transport costs, 1972–83. (Source: GB. Parliament, 1984, p. 34.)

half-fare concessions to the elderly and 1 million in areas with less generous concessions. Expenditure on providing concessionary fares varied from nil to £25 per head of the elderly population (DoT 1977; GB. Parliament 1979c).

Such geographical variation in concessionary bus fares for the elderly reflects the lack of a comprehensive national policy. In the 1970s government policy documents endorsed the principle of subsidies to ensure 'a reasonable degree of mobility' for all members of the population (see Chapter 3), and in the 1983 general election, the Labour Party proposed that half-fare concessions should be introduced universally for pensioners; under the present government it remains the responsibility of the local authority to determine what the appropriate level of concession should be.

There are important financial constraints on the capacity of local bus operators to introduce concessionary schemes. The bus industry is increasingly dependent on subsidy to maintain economic viability in the face of falling revenue from the farebox, which makes it more difficult to use income from those paying full fares to subsidize concessions to other passengers. For example, in 1972, the level of stage receipts at 1980 prices was £1,354.8 million, but by 1982 this had declined to £1,183.6 million. Revenue support over the same period, standardized to 1980 prices, increased from £31 million to

£435 million. The public operators in 1982/3 obtained 28 per cent of their total income from revenue support and 10 per cent from concessionary fares subsidies (Table 3.5) (GB. Parliament 1984: 35).

While the costs of provision of subsidized bus services for elderly people can be calculated fairly easily, the social need for such provision is more difficult to assess. Poor public transport may have an impact on accessibility of a range of local services, and measurement of access opportunity has been the object of several geographical studies, particularly in rural areas of Britain.

For example, Moseley and Spencer (1978) have calculated access opportunity for shopping facilities in rural Norfolk on the basis of the frequency of bus services, the walking distance to the facility or the bus stop, the trip duration, and start and finish times for the journey in relation to acceptable time of arrival at the destination. On this basis, they estimated that 10 per cent of the adult residents in the North Walsham area were without reasonable opportunity of access to a local foodstore, and 37 per cent did not have access to a chemist.

In the Cotswolds, Smith and Grant (1982) showed that 68 per cent of elderly people were completely dependent on public transport, and that 80 per cent of elderly bus passengers made their journey for a shopping trip. Elderly people were more likely than younger people to make use of village stores, although the average price of goods was higher than in the major shopping centres. While this might reflect a preference for the type of service provided by a small local facility, it was also found that elderly people were more likely to consider inadequate public transport a disadvantage of rural life. In more urban settings the introduction of concessionary fare schemes has also been found to result in changes in travel patterns of elderly people, and different use of local services (Skelton 1977, 1982). It seems likely that, for elderly people in these studies, spatial behaviour and use of amenities reflects repressed preferences because of constraints in mobility which limited access to spatial resources (Peace 1982).

Health facilities are also important for the elderly population, and physical access to doctor's surgeries, clinics, and hospitals may be a factor which influences use of these services, particularly in rural areas (Ritchie, Jacoby, and Bone 1981; Curtis 1980; Phillips 1979). Haynes and Bentham (1979) have shown that for younger people in rural Norfolk general practitioner consultations and outpatients attendances were less common among those living in remote rural settlements, compared to more accessible rural places. Elderly people were more likely to make use of branch surgeries for consultations with their doctor. Hospital visits were much less often made by the elderly living in inaccessible areas, although the impact of access on hospitalization rates among the elderly may be offset by provision of ambulance and domiciliary services (ibid.) .

The problem of access to health care for the elderly illustrates how in sparsely populated areas, especially where public transport is poor, there are additional costs involved in making the service accessible to users. Doctors receive additional remuneration for patients on their lists who live far from the surgery, and the costs in terms of mileage per patient of ambulance services, domiciliary nursing, and health visiting in rural areas are comparatively high. Equally, the costs of providing domiciliary social services, such as home help, will be affected by the travel costs of reaching clients in a widely dispersed population.

Thus the provision of public transport, especially in more remote areas and areas with large elderly populations, is a factor which is significant to local authority activities not only because of the cost of providing subsidies to support less profitable bus services and concessionary fares to the elderly, but also because of the additional costs which must be borne by other sectors of the welfare services to make services accessible to clients (Curtis 1980). The welfare service costs of physical accessiblity will vary geographically according to the spatial mobility of the population, population density, and the distribution of facilities in relation to the population they serve.

Housing needs of the elderly

The housing needs of the elderly underline the effects of life cycle on housing requirements and choice of residential location. Murdie's model of urban structure (Murdie, 1969; Carter, 1972) stresses the importance of stage in family formation in determining housing requirements and the residential patterning of the city. Bourne (1981), shows that age and family status influence intra-urban housing markets. With increasing age, people typically need less residential space due to what has been termed the 'empty nest' effect as children grow up and leave home. They may seek a location further removed from centres of economic activity, as access to workplace ceases to be a factor governing choice of a home; and a more supportive or sheltered residential environment may be sought as their physical capacity to manage the home becomes more limited.

Not only do elderly people have special housing requirements, but they also appear to be more likely than younger people to live in housing with poor amenities. Many are unsuitably housed in view of their physical and medical needs. For example, Table 5.2 shows that, in general, elderly people are more likely to lack such amenities as a bath and WC and to live in overcrowded accommodation. Tenure

Table 5.2   Housing characteristics of elderly households compared
with all households in Britain: 1981

Housing characteristic	All households (%)	Households with elderly members only (%)
Housing amenities		
lacking a bath	1.9	4.1
lacking a WC	2.7	5.0
with more than 1		
person per room	4.3	5.2
Housing tenure		
owner occupied	56	48
local authority rented	33	36
privately rented		
unfurnished	6	11

Source: OPCS, 1984a.

patterns also differ, as elderly people on average include a higher
proportion of council tenants than younger people, and they rely more
heavily on the unfurnished rented sector of the housing market.

Thus, although the proportion of elderly people who are council
tenants varies between local authorities, in general the elderly are an
important group of clients for the housing departments of local
authorities. A Green Paper in 1977 encouraged local authorities to
build to meet local housing needs more effectively, especially for the
elderly (DoE 1977). This often involves the creation of new types of
housing, particularly sheltered housing or warden-assisted flats.
Department of the Environment guidelines suggest that there should
be fifty places in warden-assisted dwellings per 1,000 pensionable
population, but in many areas the provision is considerably below this
and needs to be increased. For example, the Greater London Council
estimated in 1981 that it needed to increase the number of places from
current levels of about 20,000 to between 50,000 and 90,000.

At least until recently, the private and voluntary sector have not
been able to contribute very effectively towards meeting the needs of
the elderly. The elderly typically require small homes and flats, but
the private building industry has been slow to respond to these requirements. For example, in 1978, 33 per cent of new local authority dwellings constructed in England had one bedroom, compared with only 4
per cent of privately built homes (Barnard 1982). In the same year,
50 per cent of local authority housing was built as flats, compared

with only 10 per cent of privately constructed units (CSO 1983: table 3.5). Balchin (1985: 134,138) has pointed out that Housing Associations have also proved rather ill-adapted to meeting the needs of the elderly for sheltered accommodation because they are less experienced in this field than in meeting general housing needs. The inner city housing with which housing associations typically are concerned was often unsuitable for the elderly, and the relative cost to housing associations of providing sheltered housing was higher than for general housing schemes. Therefore, the elderly form a group which is particularly likely to need local authority housing provision.

Residential care for the elderly

Social service provision for the elderly by local authorities includes accommodation in residential homes for elderly people who are no longer able to live independently in private households. This is a statutory duty of local authorities under Part III of the National Assistance Act 1948, and is therefore often referred to as 'Part III' accommodation. About 5 per cent of the total pensionable population live in institutions, and most of these live in residential homes provided by local authorities, or in private residential homes which may be paid for by local authority. Some are accommodated in long-term medical institutions.

The numbers of elderly in residential accommodation have grown considerably over recent decades. In 1959 about 71,000 aged 65 and over were in such institutions in England and Wales. By 1970 the number in England was 106,000 and in 1981 117,000. In 1981, 103,000 lived in homes run by local authorities, and 14,000 were in voluntary or private homes in places paid for by the local authorities. In addition, the private and voluntary sector provided residential places directly for about 60,000 people. In 1981 the total number of places for the elderly in local authority homes in the UK was about 122,000, and this figure remained constant through 1982 and 1983. However, under the policies of the present government which encourage provision by the non-public sectors (GB. Parliament 1981), the level of voluntary and private residential provision to the elderly has expanded considerably. In 1981 the total UK capacity was about 65,000 places, rising to 69,000 in 1982 and to 76,000 in 1983 (CSO 1983).

The characteristics of elderly residents in these institutions has also changed. Residential accommodation for the elderly provided by local authorities was not originally intended to be for the frail and ill. However, as pressure is mounting on health service facilities which cannot provide for the growing number of very elderly people with

93

high disability and dependency levels, so residential homes are having to accept a growing number of very elderly and frail residents. A survey conducted in 1981 by the Personal Social Services Research Unit, University of Kent (Darton 1984) showed that the average age for residents in old people's homes was 80 years. In local authority homes 37 per cent of residents were ambulant, 60 per cent were continent, and 45 per cent were mentally alert. A similar survey in 1971 had indicated a lower level of disablement (Table 5.3). The level of dependency in private and voluntary homes had increased even more dramatically over the ten-year period, although the proportion of residents who were ambulant, continent, and mentally alert was still higher than for local authority homes in 1981 (Table 5.3).

Table 5.3   Results from two surveys of incapacity among residents of homes for the elderly in England and Wales

	In local authority homes		In private homes	
	1971	*1981*	*1971*	*1981*
%age residents who were				
Ambulant	49	37	70	43
Continent	71	60	81	59
Mentally alert	56	45	74	50

Source: Darton, 1984.

Thus it seems that local authority homes have a particularly high proportion of very disabled elderly residents, and that in all homes the burden of care for these very dependent residents is increasing. This has implications for the costs to local authorities of staffing and equipping residential homes to provide adequate care. There is also concern that local authorities may not have the capacity to inspect private homes to ensure good standards.

The level of provision of residential homes varies from one part of the country to another. At the regional level, in 1980 the total rate of provision was about 17 places/1,000 elderly people in England as a whole, ranging from 15/1,000 in the south-west to 19/1,000 in the north. Within regions the level of provision differs more widely, and levels of residential care tend to be higher in metropolitan and urban areas than in rural local authorities (Bebbington and Davies 1982: table 16.2).

The pattern of provision of residential homes by the different sectors of the welfare economy is also very variable in space. A survey of local authorities in 1985 showed considerable differences ı the proportion of residential accommodation in public sector homes provided by the local authority), and in private and in voluntary omes (Peace 1986).

While at the national scale the growth of the private sector has been reatly influenced by changes in political ideology and policy, other actors appear to come into play to determine the extent to which the rivate sector has expanded in particular areas. Figure 5.3 shows, for xample, the proportion of residential accommodation for the elderly rovided in three London boroughs, all of which were under Conservative administrations. The relative significance of the private nd voluntary sector is different in each case. Phillips and Vincent 1986) have shown that, in Devon, new private residential homes are oncentrated in holiday resorts such as Torbay and Torquay. In these ⱷwns it is particularly the neighbourhoods with large Victorian villas uitable for conversion to residential homes which have seen rapid evelopment of private provision. Historical provision by local uthorities and voluntary organizations, the availability of suitable uildings for conversion into private homes, and the demand from the ⱷcal elderly population for private provision seem therefore to be actors which combine to affect the pattern of private residential ccommodation for elderly people at the local scale. The interaction f these effects may lead to over-concentration of residential homes ı some districts, and local authorities may need to impose planning estrictions if large numbers of residential homes are seen to create emographic imbalance in the community, or if the health and social eeds of elderly residents cannot be adequately met (Murray 1985).

Thus, although all elderly people in need are entitled to Part III esidential care, the type of provision which will be made for such eople varies geographically, according to the activities of the public, rivate, and voluntary sector. The proportion of elderly entering esidential care also varies (Figure 5.4). This is partly due to haracteristics of the elderly population which affect their dependency ıd needs for institutional care, but it also reflects local authority ɔlicies, and the extent to which domiciliary care is provided to the lderly in their own homes, in order to defer the point at which eception into an institution becomes inevitable.

ommunity care for the elderly

urrent government policies place emphasis on services designed to ɛduce the proportion of frail elderly and chronically ill people who ɛe hospitalized, by providing community care services to sick and isabled people in their own homes (DHSS 1981). These include ɛrsonal social services such as home help, meals on wheels, day

95

centres and clubs, laundry services, sitters-in, visitors and social workers; and also health services such as domiciliary nursing and health visiting to the elderly. The level of provision of these services varies a good deal from one part of the country to another. Table 5.4 for example, shows how the home help and meals on wheels service varies between regions. Local authorities differ widely and the charges made to clients are also variable.

At the national scale, these differences between local authorities cannot be totally explained in terms of variation in the need of the elderly population (Bebbington and Davies 1982; Bebbington *et al* 1988), although Pinch (1980, 1985: 50–60) has shown comparatively high positive correlation in London between social service provision to the elderly and social deprivation measured by a more general

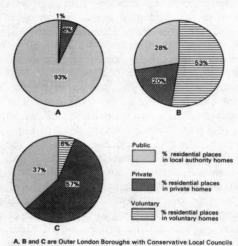

A, B and C are Outer London Boroughs with Conservative Local Councils

Figure 5.3 Residential provision for the elderly in three London boroughs; proportions provided in public, private and voluntary sector homes: 1985. (Source: Peace, 1986.)

social conditions index. There is general agreement that local political factors have an influence on levels of provision (Davies, Barton, and McMillan 1971; Bebbington and Davies 1982; Pinch 1980) and on charging for services (Judge, Ferlie and Smith 1982; Dexter and Harbert 1983). Thus the availability and cost of services for elderly people will depend not only on local needs, but also on the political composition of the local authority and the ideologies of care which are adopted by the Social Service Committees.

Table 5.4 Home help services to the elderly in regions of the UK: 1980

Regions	Home help cases per 1,000 households with persons of pensionable age
North	193.1
Yorkshire and Humberside	199.2
East Midlands	158.8
East Anglia	136.8
South-east	141.9
South-west	131.1
West Midlands	170.3
North-west	167.2
Wales	162.1
Scotland	130.7 (1979 data)
Northern Ireland	209.7 (estimated)

Source: Central Statistical Office, *Regional Trends*, 1982.

Equally, the regional level of provision of domiciliary nursing services between health authorities is variable, as shown in Table 5.5. Many observers have commented that provision of community health services often does not correspond to patterns of need in the population (Pinch 1980; London Health Planning Consortium 1981). Indeed the policies for development of community care have been criticized for shifting the costs of care for the chronically ill from health authorities to social services, who are responsible for a large part of the support services which are necessary to maintain elderly people at home. The elderly are one of the client groups for whom joint planning of health and social care is essential. However, the discussion in Chapter 3 has shown that the level of development of joint planning is very variable between authorities. A major improvement in co-ordination of services remains to be achieved in most authorities before fully integrated provision to the elderly at home can be possible.

The introduction of community care policies and variations in levels of statutory domiciliary care provision have a considerable impact not only on the elderly, but on friends and relatives who care for them at home. In the UK the present government sees the informal sector as a major contributor to care in the community (GB. Parliament 1981d). Several commentators have drawn attention to the social and financial burden of caring for sick, elderly relatives. One study showed

Table 5.5 Domiciliary nursing provision in regions of the UK: 1986

Regional health authority	Nurses/10,000 population over 65 years	Nurses/10,000 population of all ages
Northern	25.0	3.8
Yorkshire and Humberside	19.9	3.1
Trent	21.9	3.3
East Anglia	18.2	2.9
North West Thames	20.2	2.8
North East Thames	17.7	2.7
South East Thames	20.0	3.4
South West Thames	19.5	3.2
Wessex	18.7	3.2
Oxford	22.0	2.8
South Western	17.2	3.0
West Midlands	21.2	3.0
Mersey	22.4	3.3
North Western	26.6	4.1
Wales	26.9	4.3
Scotland	33.0	4.8
Northern Ireland	32.0	3.8
UK	22.4	3.4

Source: Central Statistical Office, *Regional Trends*, 1988.

that the economic cost to a carer of giving up work altogether wa estimated to be on average £120 per week in 1980, and half of the families surveyed had lost earnings averaging £42 per week (Equa Opportunities Commission 1982).

Spatial variation in welfare needs and planning for the elderly

The elderly are a group which illustrates very clearly the geographica and social aspects of accessibility of public services. They are a significant and growing sector of the population who make heavy demands on the welfare services. While they have some politica power over local and national political decisions through the democratic system, they are an economically (and often socially dependant group not directly involved in the provision of tne public services which they consume. The spatial distribution of the elderly results in large elderly populations in certain parts of the country while in other areas relatively high proportions of people in extreme old age or living alone without family support can also present a particular challenge to local health and social service departments.

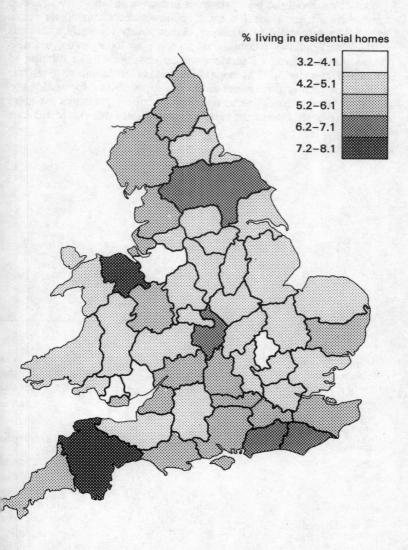

Figure 5.4 The percentage of the population over 75 years living in residential accommodation, by counties of England and Wales. (Source: as Figure 5.3.)

99

Decisions about the best pattern of provision for these clients raise some difficult questions for social policy-makers and society as a whole. The decentralized system of responsibility for welfare services to the elderly allows flexibility of response to local needs, but also means that provision of services varies considerably in relation to political factors as well as population needs. Furthermore, given the division of administrative and financial responsibility for health and social services, a co-ordinated response to current pressures for more community-based care of the elderly is particularly difficult to achieve.

Chapter six

Welfare provision for ethnic minorities

The identity and distribution of ethnic minorities

Ethnicity is a difficult concept to define. The other priority groups considered in this book are identified by the single criterion of age. However, ethnic minorities may be distinguished from the 'indigenous' population in the UK because they are foreign-born, speak a different language, have a distinctive cultural background, follow a particular religion, or belong to a particular racial type.

One of the obstacles to obtaining an appropriate indicator of ethnic minority status in the British population is the lack of statistical information. The last Census of population contained no question on ethnic background, apart from country of birth, because of the difficulties which had been encountered in finding a suitable question acceptable to respondents (Sillitoe 1987). For more detailed information about ethnic minorities at the national or metropolitan level, we therefore rely on sample surveys such as the *Labour Force Survey* (OPCS 1986b), the *National Dwelling and Housing Survey* (DoE 1978), and a series of studies by the Policy Studies Institute (Brown 1984).

The differentiating features most commonly used in studies of ethnic minorities are country of birth and skin colour. Many people belonging to ethnic minorities are immigrants to this country, and immigrant status is often used as an indicator of ethnicity, partly because this information is available for all parts of Britain from the decennial Census. On this basis, it is possible to recognize many heterogeneous ethnic groups such as those from Ireland, New Commonwealth countries and Pakistan, Old Commonwealth countries, the European Economic Community, and other countries in Europe. However, the fact of being an immigrant to Britain is not always a clear indicator of racial or cultural group. The *Labour Force Survey* for 1985 showed that 57 per cent of all those born outside the UK, and 20 per cent of New Commonwealth and Pakistan immigrants, classified themselves as 'white' rather than belonging to a foreign ethnic group (OPCS 1986b: table 5). Furthermore, 2 per cent of those born in the UK considered themselves to belong to a 'non-white' ethnic group (ibid.: table 4).

This growing group of the British-born population who have a non-British family background are sometimes referred to as 'second-generation immigrants', a term condemned as worse than meaningless by Ahmed (1984). The use of immigrant status to distinguish ethnic minorities in the UK illustrates the tendency for such terms to acquire discriminatory and racist implications, and highlights the sensitivity of the issue of ethnic classification and discrimination, discussed by many authors including Rathwell and Philips (1986: 1–7), Donovan (1986), and Brown (1984: 4–6).

An alternative assessment of ethnicity often used in national sample surveys is self-classification as either 'white' or belonging to a number of 'non-white' national/cultural groups such as West Indian, Indian, Pakistani, Bengali, Arab, Chinese, and so on. These categories imply a multi-dimensional definition of ethnicity incorporating skin colour, which is one of the attributes which most obviously distinguishes many ethnic minorities. In the following discussion reference is often made to the distinction between the 'black' and 'white' populations in the UK. The black population includes a diversity of ethnic groups, and in many studies it comprises particularly those of West Indian, Asian, and African ethnic background. Some of the issues discussed here are also relevant to people who are less recognizable in terms of skin colour, such as those from Irish, Jewish, or Greek communities, as well as to Chinese and other oriental groups. In 1981 the Census showed that about 6 per cent of the population of the UK was foreign-born, of which approximately 3 per cent came from the New Commonwealth and Pakistan and 2 per cent from Ireland and other European countries. The *Labour Force Survey*, which covers annually about one in every 350 British households, shows that on average during 1983–5 4.3 per cent of respondents were classified as 'non-white', and 3.4 per cent of all respondents were West Indian, Indian, Pakistani, Bangladeshi, or African (OPCS 1986b: table 1).

The geographical concentration of ethnic minorities in particular parts of the country is significant for local welfare services. Table 6.1 shows how the proportion of foreign-born population varies regionally, with particular concentrations in urban areas such as Greater London, West Yorkshire, West Midlands, and Greater Manchester. Data from the *Labour Force Survey* for 1985 showed that 68 per cent of those in the 'non-white' ethnic groups lived in the areas of the old metropolitan counties. For West Indians the proportion was 80 per cent, and for Pakistanis and Bangladeshis over 70 per cent (ibid.: table 3).

As shown in Table 6.1, the residential concentration of ethnic minorities is very variable, even within regions.

Table 6.1 Geographical variations in the concentration of ethnic minorities in the UK: 1981

Region	Metropolitan area	Percentage born:	
		Outside the UK	In New Commonwealth and Pakistan
North		1.9	0.68
	Tyne and Wear	2.1	0.78
Yorkshire and Humberside		4.4	2.05
	South Yorkshire	2.7	1.23
	West Yorkshire	6.4	3.53
East Midlands		5.1	2.62
East Anglia		5.4	1.32
South-east		11.0	5.14
	Greater London	18.2	9.54
South-west		4.0	1.33
West Midlands		6.7	3.80
	West Midlands	9.8	6.25
North-west		4.3	1.73
	Greater Manchester	5.8	2.48
	Merseyside	2.7	0.72
Wales		2.5	0.73
Scotland		2.8	0.79
Northern Ireland		4.7	<0.50

Source: Central Statistical Office, *Regional Trends*, 1982, table 2.5, p. 50.

In 1975 the government produced a White Paper on racial discrimination (GB. Parliament 1975), which found evidence of discrimination with respect to employment, education, housing, and goods and services. Following the recommendations of this report, the Commission for Racial Equality (CRE) was established, and the Race Relations Act came into force in 1976. Under this legislation local authorities and similar public bodies have a duty to make appropriate arrangements to ensure that their functions are carried out 'with due regard' for the need to eliminate unlawful racial discrimination, and to promote equality of opportunity and good relations between persons of different racial groups.

Recent civil disturbances in Brixton and Tottenham (London), Toxteth (Liverpool), St Paul's (Bristol), and Handsworth (Birmingham) have also stimulated reports on the inequalities underlying social tensions associated with immigrant communities (GB. Parliament 1981a; Gifford 1986). For example, Lord Scarman concluded from his investigation of the Brixton disorders in 1981 that three areas of disadvantage emerged from the evidence he had received: housing, education, and employment. The Home Affairs Committee (1986) report on Bangladeshis in Britain similarly stressed living conditions as a major problem for that group. These have particular relevance to the provision of welfare services that we consider in this book, and the implications for local authority housing, education, and the health services are now discussed.

Considerable emphasis is now placed in pubic service policy and planning on the provision of services to ethnic minorities, especially in urban areas. The issues raised relate not only to the relatively poor levels of well-being of ethnic minorities, but also to the ways in which the structure and operation of public service organizations may themselves be discriminatory. The problem of institutionalized racism is one which is referred frequently in this chapter. Concern over racial discrimination in welfare services involves the interrelated problems of access for clients to services (or the quality of services) and of employment patterns, which affect the role of ethnic minorities working in the services.

Black populations and public housing

There is a long tradition in social geography of studies which have examined the residential patterning of different racial groups. Some of these, which relate particularly to Britain, are reviewed, for example, by Jones (1979), Jones and Eyles (1977: ch. 7), Jackson and Smith (1981), and Peach (1982). Models of urban structure (Murdie 1969) and of the determinants of urban housing markets (Bourne 1981), which emphasize ethnicity as one of the important factors, are relevant for the UK as well as North American cities. The typical pattern is one of extreme segregation and concentrations of immigrants and ethnic minority populations in certain areas of cities, which are often areas of high socio-economic deprivation.

Jackson (1985) has pointed out that geographers are increasingly concerned to examine the explanations for these high concentrations of ethnic minorities. In part, the pattern seems to reflect the social distance between social groups in British society; and it also clearly demonstrates discrimination in access to housing for black populations. Access to housing contributes to the position of ethnic minorities in the socio-economic structure of the UK and has implications for public service provision.

Blacks are likely to be disadvantaged in the private sector of housing markets for various reasons (Bourne 1981; GB. Parliament 1975). They require housing in urban areas, where the housing supply is often limited, and since they are often recent immigrants with constrained spatial mobility, their knowledge of alternative housing markets and their area of search are likely to be restricted.

Their position may be exacerbated by the activities of 'gatekeepers' in the private housing market, who seek to reduce what they see as the risks of racial change in the residential population. For example, building societies and other mortgage lenders may be less readily disposed to lend to black home owners. Brown (1984: table 50) reported that 77 per cent of white owner occupiers had building society mortgages, compared with 68 per cent of Asians and 65 per cent of West Indians. Black home owners were more likely to borrow from local authorities or (in the case of Asians) banks to buy property. It might be argued that black home buyers are more likely to be purchasing properties they had rented from local authorites, which might account for the higher proportion of local authority homes. Nevertheless, the figures suggest that the housing market and home loan system typically operate differently for blacks and whites.

The PSI survey also showed that white households were more likely than black households to be renting accommodation privately, especially unfurnished property (ibid.: 97–9). It seems likely that this is partly because landlords discriminate against black tenants (McIntosh and Smith 1974).

Because of their relative disadvantage in the private housing market, blacks have particular needs for local authority housing. This is reflected in the higher proportion of council tenants among the black population, especially West Indians. The PSI survey for 1982 showed that, in the inner city areas of London, Birmingham, and Manchester, 42 per cent of whites and of Asians rented their homes from the council, compared with 59 per cent of West Indians (Brown 1984: 99).

The housing status of black people is therefore poorer, in terms of Rex's (1971) classification than for whites (see Chapter 1). Furthermore, they tend to occupy housing of a poorer physical standard. Evidence for this from the PSI survey is shown in Table 6.2, indicating higher proportions of blacks in housing which is overcrowded, lacking amenities, and perceived to be unsatisfactory. It appears that the procedures operated by local authorities in allocating rented property, and home improvement grants, may contribute towards the local residential distribution of ethnic groups in Britain, and the poorer average standard of housing occupied by black households.

Table 6.2   Variations in housing conditions for different ethnic groups in the UK: 1982

	Ethnic group :		
	White	*Asian*	*West Indian*
%age of those in social class I, in housing which was:			
owner occupied	86	73	78
rented from the council	10	14	10
%age of those in social class II, in housing which was:			
owner occupied	21	72	33
rented from the council	66	24	53
%age in shared dwellings	1	5	4
mean no. of persons/room	0.5	1.0	0.8
%age with 1.5(+) persons/ room	1	12	3
%age lacking bath/hot water supply/inside WC	5	7	5
%age very satisfied with their home	56	41	30
For those renting from the council: %age allocated a home because:			
on the waiting-list	50	52	38
homeless	6	23	23
demolition/decant case	15	11	18
medical reasons	6	5	6

Source: Brown, 1984.

In Chapter 1 it was observed that council housing allocation policies have been shown to discriminate between different socio-economic groups. There is also evidence that allocation procedures discriminate between blacks and whites. Rex and Moore (1967) showed, in Birmingham, how access to council housing of the best quality was regulated by a five-year waiting period and by the recommendations of housing visitors. These procedures tended to discriminate against New Commonwealth immigrants. Henderson and Karn (1984) also report that the housing allocation procedures in Birmingham are discriminatory, and a similar situation has been revealed in Nottingham (Simpson 1984).

In London a study was commissioned by the CRE to examine

housing allocation in Hackney, where 25 per cent of the population is black (mainly West Indian) and 60 per cent live in council rented accommodation (CRE 1984a, 1984b; Harrison 1984). The study showed that ethnicity could be identified from the files on a high proportion of council housing applicants, although the identification of ethnic group was not officially recorded. More blacks (60 per cent) than whites (47 per cent) could be identified, and 38 per cent of tenants who were black were specifically described as such. Although blacks apparently did not have to wait longer for housing, those on waiting-lists who moved into council housing were more likely than whites to be in older properties, in flats rather than houses or maisonettes, and in properties on upper-floor levels. The study also showed that 45 per cent of the tenants on two estates with poorer-quality housing in the borough were black, compared with an average of 15 per cent for Hackney as a whole.

The differences in the allocation patterns did not seem to be explained in terms of family type, rent arrears, or area preferences. Medical references were provided for a larger proportion of whites, although the type of housing they received did not seem to relate to the type of housing required, and housing officers' notes on standards of housekeeping and the grade of housing appropriate for the applicant were less favourable for blacks. The CRE recommended a review of policies and practices of housing allocation, a systematic method of recording ethnicity, and improved staff training. Duncan (1976, p.18) sums up effectively the position with regard to blacks and housing: 'Blacks do not create problems in particular areas, but are received there because of existing problems in the area and their disadvantage in housing'

It thus appears that local authorities with large proportions of black residents are likely to have particularly heavy demands for council housing from this group because of the poorer access to adequate housing for these ethnic minorities. Apparently, local authorities' housing departments also have to make efforts to improve their own institutional procedures to ensure that black clients are not unfairly discriminated against. This may require additional resources for local authority housing in some urban authorities, and it is certainly a matter demanding political and administrative sensitivity to the needs and demands of the local population.

Education and employment for ethnic minorities

As we have seen in Chapter 4, large immigrant populations and non-English-speaking children were viewed as a factor in educational priority. Funds for early educational services were therefore directed partly towards minority populations.

In this chapter we consider, in more detail, the outcomes of education, taking up the issues about inequality referred to in Chapter 1, and consider the position of black children specifically. Several reports have examined the educational achievement of ethnic minorities. For example, the Rampton Report on West Indian children in UK schools highlighted the particularly poor outcome of school education for this group. The report (GB. Parliament 1981b: 6–10)included evidence from a study by the DES carried out in 1978 in six local education authorities (LEAs) where about half of school-leavers were from ethnic minorities. The results (Table 6.3) show that, compared with England as a whole, the levels of academic achievement were lower in the schools studied; however, West Indians were even less likely than 'other' students to attain good examination results at O-level, or to obtain A-level qualifications. They were also less likely to go on to university, although more went into other forms of further education, and their prospects of employment on leaving school were apparently poorer. The effect did not apply equally to all black children since the Asian pupils achieved better at school than the West Indians.

Even among broad ethnic groupings, the picture is complex, for example, Bangladeshis do less well than other Asians. Home circumstances and parental expectations probably play an important role. Bagley, Bart, and Wong (1979) showed that West Indian children from middle-class families achieved better than those from less privileged backgrounds within the same ethnic group.

The Rampton Report identified several factors in the education system contributing to under-achievement by West Indians, including poorer pre-school educational experience; difficulties of reading and language; inappropriate curriculum, books, and other teaching materials; an examination system which disadvantaged West Indians; racism in schools; and poor links between the school and the community. The recommendations included more co-ordination, improvement, and expansion of services for pre-school children in areas with large West Indian populations; improved liaison with parents and dissemination of information to parents about pre-school services and progress of pupils at school; enhanced multi-lingual teaching; and the introduction of teaching materials and teaching practices which would permit more multi-cultural education.

These recommendations were reinforced by the Scarman Report on the Brixton disorders (GB. Parliament 1981a), which gave an account of the views of the West Indian population on problems in schools such as lack of discipline, failure of teachers to motivate West Indian

Table 6.3 Achievement of schoolchildren in different ethnic groups in six local education authorities in England

Measure of achievement	Percentage of school-leavers in study areas			
	Asians	West Indians	Other	All England
(No. of children)	(527)	(799)	(4,852)	(693,840)
With high grades for O-level or CSE in:				
English	21	9	29	34
Maths	20	5	19	23
5 or more subjects	18	3	16	21
With A-levels	13	2	12	13
Destination on leaving school:				
university	3	1	3	5
other further education	18	16	9	14
employment	54	65	77	74
unknown	25	18	11	8

Source: GB. Parliament, 1981b, pp. 6–10.

children, and a tendency to write them off as unlikely to achieve well, a lack of contact between home and school, and a lack of sensitivity among teachers or in the curriculum to the cultural background and traditions of West Indians.

More recently, the Swann Report, *Education for All* (GB. Parliament 1985b) has tended to play down the problem of institutionalized racism in schools, although it favoured a pluralist model for teaching, embracing both multi-ethnic teaching and provision for 'special needs' of ethnic minorities (see *New Society*, 23 March 1985). However, a study carried out at the University of Keele, on twenty-three schools in Bedford, Birmingham, Bradford, and London, suggested that the lower achievement of children of Afro-Caribbean descent was affected by expectations and attitudes of teaching staff. Thus, it appears, racism has become to some extent institutionalized within the education system, and is a factor determining the outcomes of educational provision for some black children (Eggleston *et al.* 1986).

The conclusions from all these reports make depressing reading in view of the apparent failure to bring about changes in conditions in schools which will significantly improve the academic achievement of black students compared with their white peers. All the recommendations imply relatively high resource needs for education in areas with large ethnic minorities, but also suggest a need for some fundamental institutional changes. One of the changes which is clearly needed is a wider induction of teachers from ethnic minorities into some British schools, especially at the more senior levels. Thomas (1984b) points out that he was able to identify only one black headteacher of a secondary school outside London at the time he was writing.

Although some education authorities (for example, the ILEA) have shown a major commitment to multi-cultural education, this does not fully meet the requirements of some ethnic minority groups, who would prefer separate educational provision for their children. These demands are greatest in the case of some schools where the proportion of ethnic minority pupils is high. For example, in Tower Hamlets, 42 per cent of pupils in primary schools and 36 per cent of those in secondary schools were of Bangladeshi parents in 1985/6.

Pluralist and multi-cultural models of education are appropriate in Britain's inner cities, and will increasingly prevail. However, such policies do raise some difficult social and political questions for LEAs when resources are limited. The special needs of ethnic minorities have to be set against the requirements of the majority of school-children in urban areas. Spending cuts have affected the facilities in schools throughout the UK, according to the Schools Inspectorate (HMI 1988). In the inner cities both black and white pupils achieve less well academically on average (see Chapter 1, and *New Society*, 15 March 1984); LEAs may be disinclined to be seen to be singling out a particular group of children for special treatment when the level of social deprivation is high for inner city pupils from all cultural groups. There is also the question of how far education in schools in the UK should aim to integrate children into the culture of the majority rather than reinforcing the cultural distinctiveness of minority ethnic groups. The debate over integrationist vs. pluralist models in welfare provision is considered in the conclusion to this chapter.

Finally, it is argued that no amount of positive discrimination in schools will significantly affect the later life chances of blacks unless the job opportunities for school-leavers are also improved. It is necessary to complement efforts for children at school with programmes which will improve their access to further training, especially to help them gain professional qualifications.

Health and social services for ethnic minorities

The health of ethnic minorities differs from that of the average for the UK population as a whole. The response of some health authorities is questionable, because it has tended to overemphasize diseases which are particularly common among minority ethnic groups but which affect relatively small numbers of people, and to view these patient groups as 'problems', requiring improved treatment, screening, and health education programmes (Donovan 1984). While there may be justification in such policies, they do not appear to address adequately the more widespread effects on health of ethnic minorities associated with the impact of poor living conditions, and inferior access to health care.

Epidemiological studies of general patterns of mortality have demonstrated some ethnic disparities. An analysis by Marmot, Adestein, and Bulusu (1983) has shown that Standardized Mortality Rates (SMRs) for all causes are high for women of Caribbean and Asian origin and for African immigrants generally. An examination of cause-specific mortality also shows differences between ethnic minorities and the general population. For example, heart disease is a predominant cause of death in the UK population as a whole, but it appears to be particularly common among Asians (Tunstall *et al.* 1975; Marmot, Adestein, and Bulusu 1983; Bandaranayke 1986: 94; Silman *et al.* 1985).

However, it is often difficult to disentangle the complex interrelationships between race and class and mortality. Marmot, Adestein, and Bulusu (1983) also showed that black males in non-manual social classes had higher mortality rates than whites, but the reverse was true for those in the manual occupations. There is also the possible confounding influence of the 'healthy migrant' effect, resulting in a more robust immigrant population.

The same problem of interpretation is illustrated with respect to infant mortality. Information from the Office of Population Censuses and Surveys (OPCS), summarized in Table 6.4, shows that infant and perinatal mortality was also somewhat higher for ethnic minorities, although the differentials were not as great as for social classes (see Chapter 1).

Several local studies have also investigated this question, for example, in Bradford, where Lumb, Congdon, and Lealman (1981) have investigated the apparently high rate of perinatal mortality among babies of Asian mothers, and have pointed to a number of characteristics of Asians which may be relevant, including social class differences, small stature, and frequent pregnancies at short intervals. Bandaranayke (1986: 96–7) also reports that, for Asians in Bradford,

111

Table 6.4   Perinatal and infant mortality according to mother's country of origin and the socio-economic status of the family: 1983

	Perinatal mortality rate*	Infant mortality rate*
Country of birth of mother		
UK	10.2	9.9
Bangladesh/India	13.3	11.2
West Indies	11.2	11.7
Pakistan	20.2	18.8
Africa	12.0	9.2
Social class of family		
class I	7.3	6.2
class V	12.7	12.8
All	10.4	10.0

*Perinatal mortality rate = stillbirths and deaths under 1 week of age per 1,000 births; infant mortality rate = deaths under 1 year of age per 1,000 live births.
Source: OPCS Monitor DH3 85/1, *Infant and Perinatal Mortality*, 1983.

the rate of stillbirths and infant deaths from non-handicapping conditions is not significantly higher than for whites of similar social classes, although deaths from handicapping conditions are more common among Asian infants.

The Bradford studies also show that uptake of antenatal and child health services by Asian mothers is less frequent and later than for white mothers. This finding is echoed in other local studies such as those reported by Clarke and Clayton (1983) in Leicester, and by Johnson (1986) in the West Midlands. This difference in health care behaviour raises questions about the accessibility and appropriateness of maternity and child health services for ethnic minorities.

Less common diseases which have attracted the attention of health authorities include tuberculosis, which has a particularly high incidence among Asians. The response of the medical profession has favoured the implementation of improved screening of immigrants on entry to Britain, and in the areas of highest concentration of immigrant populations (Joint Tuberculosis Committee 1978). However, other observers have suggested that the disease is more often contracted in the UK rather than imported and that poor living conditions as well as low immunization rates are to blame (Khogali 1979; Bandaranayke 1986).

Similarly, campaigns against rickets among Asians have been criticized for attempting to modify dietary practices in order to boost vitamin D intake in foods such as margarine and fatty fish (*British Medical Journal* 30 July 1979; Sheiham and Quick 1982). This seems to contradict the dietary advice offered to the population generally, which stresses reduction of fat intake. Indeed health education should be more sympathetic generally to the beneficial aspects of the diet of ethnic minorities, even though the staples are typically not those traditionally favoured by the British population (Jervis 1986).

It appears that black populations living in deprived areas, like their white neighbours, consider environmental health problems and poor access to health care to be more important than the health threat of specific diseases. For example, Lauglo (1984: table 4.3) showed that in Spitalfields (East London) local people were more concerned about rubbish disposal, poor and overcrowded housing, lack of play space for children, unemployment, lack of money, and inadequate health services than about ill-health as such. The same survey showed that 35 per cent of Asians thought that local health services were very good, compared with 62 per cent of 'English' respondents. Curtis also found evidence of this concern for environmental health issues among the black population of Tower Hamlets (Curtis 1983; Curtis and Ogden 1987).

Many critics of the health services and health education for ethnic minorities argue that the services are poorly suited to the needs of black users, and that this is partly because there is a failure to recruit black workers into the services, especially in the superior, more influential posts. A survey of staff in London hospitals is quoted in a study on this subject by the CRE (1983), to show that while nurses and ancillary staff include a high proportion of immigrant workers, clerical staff, professional technicians, and doctors were mainly British-born. Other evidence of persistant inequality in employent in the NHS has been compiled by Hughes, McNaught, and Pennell (1984).

The provision of personal social services poses similar issues to those facing the National Health Service. It has been noted that local authorities have a duty to combat racial disadvantage, and the provision of social services is one of the means at their disposal. Cheetham (1982) summarizes the issues for social work with ethnic minorities; the question of the ends and means of recording ethnic data on clients; the difficulty of assessing needs and appreciating family strengths in unfamiliar cultures; the disproportionate number of West Indian children in care; the development and adaptation of special services for minority groups; and the recruitment and training of suitable staff, especially from among the ethnic minorities.

Consideration has already been given to the implications for social service departments of the need to improve day care provision for pre-school children from ethnic minorities, and to co-ordinate more effectively with LEAs. The Community Relations Commission (1975) showed that West Indians rely relatively heavily on childminders in Lambeth, Leicester, and Manchester. Therefore, for this group, the regulation and inspection of childminders by local authorities is particularly important. In Bradford, in 1984, a black woman was awarded damages because the local authority could not provide a childminder who would accept a black child (*Guardian*, 12 October 1984).

In view of the high proportion of black children in care, the question of ethnic matching with foster parents is an important one (Parker 1980). In some areas special initiatives are necessary, as in Lambeth, where the New Black Families Unit has been set up to recruit black foster parents for black children (Arnold 1982).

As the demographic profile of immigrant communities in Britain begins to mature, there is also growing concern over how to provide for the needs of the elderly from ethnic minorities. Their needs have been investigated in several surveys, and Glendenning (1982) suggests that in addition to this sort of information, staff training and recruitment should take into account their needs (e.g. more home helps from ethnic minorities); better information should be made available on welfare rights; and the outcomes and quality of residential care for clients from ethnic minorities should be monitored.

Meeting multiple welfare needs of ethnic minorities

This chapter has shown that ethnic minorities in Britain, especially the black population, are subject to disadvantage in a number of aspects of welfare. The cumulative effects of this multiple disadvantage extends into other dimensions of life not considered in detail here. For example, there is also evidence that the ethnic populations in this country are discriminated against in the British labour market (Thomas 1984a, 1984b; Brown 1984; Hubbock and Carter 1980), and some writers have commented on the links between housing, residential mobility, and opportunities for employment (Palmer and Gleave 1981).

These inequalities of opportunity are of concern to the welfare service system in two respects. First, as already observed, the recruitment of employees in the services themselves shows a bias against blacks, conflicting with policies for equal opportunities and making it more difficult to provide services which are well suited to the needs of ethnic minority clients. Second, the high level of

n fact these are perennial issues which are the subject of constant
ebate in all countries with a hierarchical spatial administrative
tructure incorporating central and local government. Opinions about
he best approach to geographical variations in services will depend,
n part, on arguments about the relative merits of localist or centralist
nodels of provision (Bennett 1980: ch. 3; Selden 1980; Ranson, Jones
nd Walsh 1985; Jones and Stewart 1985; Pinch 1985: 32–7). Localist
nodels suggest that local administrative areas should be allowed a
arge degree of autonomy in service provision. Under this system it
nay be argued that mechanisms of public choice, negotiation, and
iscal migration will operate to create local 'service clubs', a pattern
f provision which varies to correspond to local community
equirements, and that access to services in different areas will be
quitable, even if it is not equal (Tiebout 1956; Dahl 1956;
Iirschmann 1970).

However, an equitable distribution produced by this model would
equire full and equal participation of all members of the community
n decision-making and full mobility of the population, allowing them
ree choice of their residential location. Neither condition is realistic.
Chapter 6 has shown that for ethnic minorities choice of residential
ocation is constrained. For the elderly, there is also evidence reported
n Chapter 5, that elderly people may not be satisfied with their
esidential location in every respect, and that their use of local services
nay reflect repressed preferences.

The localist model also ignores the effects of community
lifferences in ability to pay and of spill-over effects, which will affect
he capacity of different 'service clubs' to make the type of provision
hey require, and to keep provision exclusive to the 'members' resident
vithin its jurisdiction. The localist model assumes that local
government policies and the ways that these are implemented are well
uned to the needs and wishes of the local population. Weberian
nterpretations, however, see local government as bureaucratic, seeking
o perpetuate their organization as a priority goal rather than
esponding to the needs of the wider community (Pinch 1985: 36;
Weber 1958). A 'managerial' interpretation (Williams 1978) would
uggest that in a highly decentralized welfare system small numbers
f 'gatekeepers' will exercise considerable control over the distribution
f resources for welfare. If their procedures and policies are insensitive
o public choice or are not flexible enough to respond to varying
ieeds, public welfare provision may not reflect the demands of local
ommunities. A further problem for social justice nationally is that the
ursuit of a purely localist model of provision is likely to lead to an
ndesirable degree of spatial inequality between different areas of the
ountry.

The contrasting centralist model advocates equalization of servic provision between local administrative areas by the application c standards of provision and expenditure laid down by centra government, and by mechanisms for redistribution of resource between local areas. Those supporting a more centralist scheme woul point out that it facilitates the maintenance of universal minimur standards, below which services are not allowed to fall. It also allow for regional redistribution of central welfare resources to counterac the resource–need disparity (the uneven spatial distribution o vulnerable groups is often inversely related to the availability o wealth in the local community to provide for them). A mor centralized system can help to prevent corruption and ensure th application of superior levels of expertise and technical facilities t aid welfare planning.

However, a highly centralized system risks becoming insensitive t local needs and being inefficient and ineffective because it lacks th flexibility to use resources in the manner best suited to local condition It is debatable whether a centralist model can ensure better represent ation for minority groups with special needs, although this might b true for groups which are too spatially dispersed to affect local policie but can be collectively successful in lobbying central government.

The Layfield Report discussed the changing nature of central–loca government relations in the UK, in the 1970s (GB. Parliament 1976b ch. 5). A drift towards a more centralized system was noted, arisin, partly from political pressures on central government to ensure bette minimum standards and greater universality for important services lik education and welfare, and also from the inflexibility of the local ta base, which made it necessary to increase the level of financ.al inpu from central government to fund local services.

The Layfield Committee considered the outcomes which could b expected if the trend for more centralization were allowed to continue National government would be faced increasingly with the problen of weighing public service expenditure requirements against othe government expenditure, and would control local governmen spending more closely, not only the total level of spending but als over the way that resources were used. Local authorities would b likely to adopt increasingly the role of pressure groups seeking mor resources. The Committee also considered how far local governmen would be able to retain powers of policy-making and planning an influence central government policy. A more elaborate system of link between central and local tiers of government would be necessary with a new forum for central–local government liaison, a more effective role for associations of authorities, and perhaps a stronge regional tier of organization of some government departments.

The Layfield Committee took the view that if a more decentralized structure were required, action would be necessary to reverse the trend towards centralization. The possibility was considered of resorting to a compromise 'half-way house' solution in which local authorities would take sole responsibility for 'local' services and central government would be concerned with non-local services. However, it was argued that national standards would need to be applied for the services which require greatest resource inputs (education, police, fire, social services, and transport). Thus the scope for increasing the fiscal autonomy of local government would be limited.

An alternative scenario, of greatly increased local responsibility, would be subject to all the problems of the localist model already discussed. Local authorities would have to be much more financially accountable. Local taxation would increase, and local councils would be subject to greater internal conflicts between local pressure groups. Central government would have less power to direct public planning and expenditure, and the level and quality of services would vary more in response to local political factors.

The trend towards centralization has not been reversed in the UK, in the 1980s, but has continued apace. Thus the pattern of government which seems to be emerging, as described in Chapter 3, is generally typified by a development of increased central government control enhanced by complete removal of regional government and restraint of the role of local authorities by changes to their powers and responsibilities, and constraint on public sector spending. At the same time, in some areas a trend is evident towards decentralization to the very local, neighbourhood level. The net effect is an erosion of the influence of local authorities over the pattern of public welfare provision, and the development of a fragmented system, with less democratic representation (Stoker 1988).

Local government funding: support by central government

The processes by which local services are financed also reflect the influence of central policy on local authorities and health authorities. Funding of welfare services and distribution of resources to authorities in different parts of the country must be viewed in the light of central government policies which have severely limited the revenue available for public services during the 1980s. Need and demand for services have increased due to demographic changes increasing the dependency ratio (especially the numbers of frail elderly people in the population). Technical advances in the health and welfare services have increased the potential for care and treatment, for previously intractable problems, and public expectations for the availability of services have

119

increased to reflect this new capacity. These trends combine to increase the cost of meeting the demand for welfare services, and when this is taken into account there has been, over recent years, a stagnation or reduction in average real resources made available by central government to local authorities and health authorities, even though the absolute amount of expenditure has increased.

The main sources of income for local authorities are (1) central government grants and subsidies, (2) local taxation (rates), (3) rents, fees and charges made to service users, and (4) income raised as capital and loans, etc.

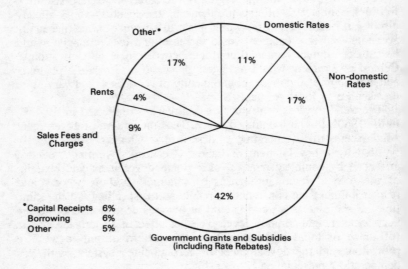

Figure 7.1 Sources of local government income in England: 1984/5. (Source: GB. Parliament, 1986.)

Income from rents, fees, and charges include revenue from commercial services and trading (docks, markets, etc.), charges for personal services such as home helps and day nurseries, and for amenities such as swimming-pools, and rent from council tenants. This income amounted to 13 per cent of all local authority income in 1984/5 (see Figure 7.1) and varied geographically according to factors such as clients' ability to pay, policies about the appropriate levels of fees and charges, and the activity of local authorities in the local economy.

The allocation of central grants and the raising of local taxes are more significant in terms of their contribution to local authority

120

income, and they involve interesting questions of central–local government relations (Bennett 1982). Figure 7.1 shows that the central government element comprised 42 per cent of income to English authorities in 1984/5. These grants are of three types: specific grants for particular purposes (e.g. fire and police services, and grants to Inner Area Partnership Authorities); supplementary grants (e.g. the transport supplementary grant, soon to be abolished); and rate support grant, which comprises 85 per cent of the total. Rate support grant is calculated in two parts: domestic relief payments to enable domestic ratepayers to pay less than commercial ratepayers, and a 'block grant' element which combines a contribution to the cost of meeting varying population needs for service provision, and compensation for the varying resources which local authorities have at their disposal due to variable rateable value of property in their area (the calculation of the needs element is discussed on p.129). Table 7.1 shows for 1980/1 how central support for regional groups of local authorities varied in England.

Each year central government fixes what proportion of the relevant local government expenditure will be met by rate support, and calculates the grant-related expenditure (GRE) which it estimates each local authority needs to provide for the population in its jurisdiction. The GRE does not necessarily reflect actual local expenditure, but where the local authority spends more than the GRE it must find the

Table 7.1 Rate and rate support grant income to local authorities in England: 1980/1

Region	Average domestic rateable value	Average domestic rates paid per hereditament	Rate support grant (£/head)	
			Resources element	Needs element
North	141	168	91	129
East Midlands	168	150	61	108
East Anglia	185	178	58	81
South-east	254	247	25	125
West Midlands	202	199	48	111
North-west	171	184	70	133
South-west	181	180	66	87
Yorkshire and Humberside	135	143	92	120

Source: Central Statistical Office. *Regional Trends*, 1982.

extra resources from local taxation. A ceiling is now placed on the amount of extra revenue which a local authority may raise in this way.

This system of central grants to local government has some advantages. It enables the provision of certain services which would otherwise be too expensive for the community to finance, but must be provided to adequate standards in the national interest (e.g. education). By redistribution it compensates some authorities which have low local revenue, high population needs, or high costs of service provision due to factors such as sparsity or high labour costs. However, the fact that local authorities depend on the rate support grant system and are therefore subject to fiscal control by central government leads to controversies, when central and local welfare policies are at odds.

Local taxation: the problem of rates

Income from rates provided 28 per cent of local government income in England in 1984/5 (Figure 7.1). The development of local authority powers to levy rates for particular types of local service has been discussed in Chapter 2. In 1925 the rating system was consolidated under the Rating and Valuation Act, which distinguished between rating authorities and precepting authorities, which levy funds indirectly from the rating authorities. In England and Wales, the rating authorities are the district councils and London boroughs. The precepting authorities are the non-metropolitan counties, and (before abolition) the metropolitan counties and Greater London Council and Inner London Education Authority. The rating system has been based on two principles: the beneficial principle of sharing the costs of service provision, and of economies of scale; and the redistributive principle to transfer resources from the wealthier members of the population to the poorer members.

Rates are levied on property units (hereditaments) which are technically occupied by a household, business, or institution. Each unit has a rateable value determined by the Inland Revenue on the basis of the market rent value of the property. The local rate, fixed annually by the rating authority, is in proportion to the rateable value. Rates are levied on most property, but that belonging to the church or in agricultural use is exempt. The larger proportion of income from local taxation is levied on non-domestic property (Figure 7.1) and domestic rates are relatively low, compared with non-domestic rates.

Rates have several advantages as a means of local taxation, being simple to administer, difficult to evade, cheap to collect, and a substantial, stable, and reliable source (GB. Parliament 1983b). Rates have some direct impact on the local community – so at least part of the electorate has a vested interest in public accountability of authorities for their spending – and may encourage mobility and availability of property on the housing market. However, the system also has some failings, and a recent government discussion document (GB. Parliament 1986) has outlined proposals for reform.

The main criticisms of rates are that they are unfair. The value of the property occupied may not correspond to income. Since only a proportion of the local population pays rates, and some of these receive rebates, the community does not have a major incentive to ensure efficient use of rates and reasonable rate levels. High non-domestic rates have been argued to be damaging to local enterprise and the local economy, although this is disputed (Midwinter and Mair 1987). Also geographical variation in rateable values is outside the control of central or local government, and is often inversely related to population need.

From the point of view of central government, the present rating system presents a political problem because of the recurrent annual wrangle which has developed over the fixing of local rates. Local councils, especially those of a different political colour from the government, have increasingly tended to raise high rates to support their social and welfare programmes. The amount of income required from the rates has increased as the level of central rate support grant declines in relation to total local authority expenditure. Central government has been driven to imposing penalties on high-spending authorities by reducing the amount they receive in rate support grant and by rate-capping, a procedure for limiting the level of rate increases. Central government now finds itself in direct, and politically embarrassing, conflict with local government over the issues of rate support grant calculation and rate-capping and would welcome a new system which would control local authority expenditure in a less controversial way. The present UK government view is that communities would bring more pressure to bear on their elected local authorities to reduce spending if a larger proportion of residents felt the financial impact of local policy directly.

Various alternatives to rates have been considered, including a local sales tax, a local income tax, and a local community tax (GB. Parliament 1983b). The first has been rejected because it would be too complex to operate, and would produce a variable and unreliable yield falling unequally on consumers and non-consumers, and local business. Clearly, local income tax would be redistributive, but would vary considerably from one part of the UK to another, would be costly to administer, and would have the politically unacceptable effect of raising the perceived tax burden.

The present government sees the third possibility of a community

123

charge as the best way foward (GB. Parliament 1986). This would operate by means of a flat rate determined by local authorities and levied on all adult residents. In 1988 community charges were being introduced in Scotland, and legislation debated in Parliament which will introduce the system to England and Wales. It is argued that it will increase accountability for spending by local government because most members of the local electorate will feel the effects of local authority expenditure, not only property-owners as at present. The charge will be unaffected by local variation in the market rent of property. The government argues that if a community charge were introduced, it would no longer be necessary to include a resources element in the rate support grant calculations, which would simplify the system of allocation of central grants. There would be some exemptions made for those on low incomes. Operational problems of maintaining a register of those liable to pay, which will be most difficult for highly mobile populations, are not considered to be insurmountable.

The introduction of community charges will result in large increases in amounts payable by many households, particularly those in authorities with currently high levels of spending. The unpopularity of these increases may cause local authorities to reduce their spending, which is precisely the effect which central government is seeking. However, those who argue against the introduction of a community charge consider that the impact of the charge will be greatest on those who are less affluent. People in rented accommodation will be paying the charge for the first time, while others owning inexpensive properities and paying lower rates will find the increase difficult to manage. Both groups may face hardship as a result, or be forced to move to an area with a lower charge. In contrast, for people owning large, expensive properties, who are, by and large, wealthier, the community charge will cost less than rates. It is therefore argued that the community charge is regressive because it is not related to ability to pay, except for those on the lowest incomes, who are exempt. The community charge is also condemned by its opponents as a 'poll tax' on the right to vote, which will cause some people to forego their democratic rights in order to evade registration and payment of the charge.

The Local Government Finance Bill, incorporating the community charge proposal, had a controversial second reading in Parliament in December 1987, and in the House of Lords in May 1988 amendments were debated which would have related the community charge more closely to ability to pay. However, these amendments were not upheld. Plans were discussed in some inner London authorities to phase in payment over a period of years to soften the blow for those who will find the charge difficult to meet. Even given any modifications introduced before the Bill becomes law, the community charge and its geographical variation is likely to become an important factor determining where families choose to live, and how local authorities respond to the needs of their populations through provision of public services.

Health service funding: resource allocation in relation to need

The administrative structure through which national health services are funded is separate from that for local authority funding (see Chapter 3). For services provided by district health authorities in hospitals, clinics, and patients' homes, the funding system operates by a process of resource allocation from the central NHS to the regional health authorities which then make subregional allocations to their constituent districts. Until 1975 funds were allocated to different parts of the UK on an incremental basis, but there was concern that provision through the National Health Service varied geographically, due mainly to the historical development of health care facilities and the distribution of teaching hospitals. The pattern often did not correspond to need in the population. For example, average levels of provision were lower in the north, where mortality rates were also high. The variation in access to services, especially hospital beds, was contrary to the principles of equality of access enshrined in the National Health Service Act 1946. The situation could be seen to correspond to Tudor-Hart's (1971) concept of the 'inverse care law', describing the spatial coincidence of medical deprivation and poor health status implying above average need for care.

In order to introduce greater equity in health funding, the Resource Allocation Working Party (RAWP) proposed a system, introduced in 1975/6, by which funds would be allocated according to 'target expenditure' based on demographic characteristics of the population (which affect the probability of illness and health care consumption) and standardized mortality rates (surrogate measures of levels of illness in the population). Growth in planned expenditure was to be restricted in regions which were spending above target, and increased to regions which were below target (DHSS 1975).

The application of the RAWP system has produced a general trend for health authority budgets to move towards target over the past ten years but this redistribution has been achieved at the expense of severe budgetary constraint in some regions in the south-east of England. Table 7.2 illustrates the target allocations, indicating the limited growth in the four Thames regions, which include the London area. The real income of health authorities is also affected by the extent to which they have been able to achieve 'efficiency savings' which the resource allocation has assumed are possible. The RAWP system is now under review, and one of the questions being addressed is whether the formula should allow additional funding for provision of health care in deprived inner city areas, especially in inner London (DHSS 1986b, Bevan and Mays 1987).

Table 7.2 Revenue allocations to regional health authorities in England: 1986/7

Regional health authority	NHS revenue increase (%), 1986/7*
Northern	6.7
Yorkshire	6.8
Trent	7.7
East Anglia	7.7
North West Thames	5.7
North East Thames	5.7
South East Thames	5.8
South West Thames	5.8
Wessex	7.7
Oxford	7.3
South Western	7.0
West Midlands	8.0
Mersey	6.0
North Western	6.4

*These increases do not allow for inflation and pay awards likely to require a 5.7 per cent increase.

The shift of resources from hospital services to community care (see Chapter 3) complicates the picture since this often implies a requirement for additional funding for new care initiatives. It is argued that the growth of community care will tend to shift the cost of care of the chronically ill away from health authorities and towards the social service departments. It seems unlikely that the limited joint finance funding from the NHS will meet the costs of implementing the community care policy. The speed with which community care policies are being put into effect makes it particularly difficult to ensure adequate standards of care for patients moving out of institutions.

While the costs of care provided by district authorities is cash-limited centrally, the provision of care and medical treatment rescribed by general practitioners is not subject to such limits. Since he GPs are contracted to the NHS, it is difficult to control their ctivities and distribution. The main means of so doing are by perating financial incentives through practice allowances, to ncourage good-quality care and establishment of new practices in nder-doctored areas. The Medical Practices Committee also controls he entry of GPs into areas which are considered to be under-doctored. he recent White Paper on primary care (GB. Parliament 1987a) uggests that the remuneration of GPs should be modified to ncourage activities such as preventative health care and health romotion, and a better quality of care in inner city areas, where verage standards are lower than in other parts of the country (London Iealth Planning Consortium 1981). It was also concluded that in letermining the spatial distribution of doctors, 'there is scope for ;iving greater emphasis to local information about medical and social ieeds' (ibid.: 18). A new practice allowance was proposed to ncourage doctors to work in deprived areas where the workload issociated with the local population is particularly high. The mplication is that there will be some enhancement of resources for ;eneral practice in deprived areas, especially in the inner city. Some neasures to reduce the stress on GPs practising in isolated rural areas vere also called for.

Thus at present there is a continuing debate in the UK over how o allocate scarce health resources most equitably between regions, and low to use them most effectively and efficiently at the local district evel. The question of how to produce indicators of health care need or the populations of different geographical areas figures significantly n these discussions.

Measuring needs: the use of area social indicators

The resource allocation systems for block grant and health service unding already considered have been developed with the objective of lirecting central resources more equitably in proportion to local population needs and the costs of service provision. These procedures lave called for methods of estimating the relative need for welfare provision of the population in the national space. The use of area ocial indicators is one of the main means of achieving this. For ipplication to all authorities in the UK, suitable indicators of relative esource needs must reflect a consistent view of the type of social need or which services should be provided, and must be available in an dentical form for local authorities throughout the country.

Geographical work in the field of social area analysis has contributed to the development of social indicators. Geographers have applied a variety of approaches to the analysis of statistical data on the spatial variation of demographic, social, and economic attributes of the population of small areas. The 'social indicator movement', first developed in the USA with the introduction of social area analysis (Shevky and Williams 1949; Shevky and Bell 1955), categorized areas of Los Angeles using statistics which were considered to relate to the economic, family, and ethnic status of the population. These three constructs were intended to reflect the theories of Louis Wirth (1938) about the processes affecting urban development.

Subsequent studies in factorial ecology used the statistical method of principal component analysis to select combinations of area statistics which would summarize in separate 'dimensions' the variation in city populations (Anderson and Egland 1961; Murdie 1969). The method was applied to data from sources such as the Census of population in several British cities, for example, London (Webber 1977a), Liverpool (Webber 1975), Cardiff (Herbert 1970). Cluster Analysis was also used as a method of summarizing variation in areal units into groups which have the least possible internal variation and are most clearly distinct from the other groups. The method was applied to Cumbria and Merseyside (Cullingford *et al* 1975; Webber 1975). Similarly, clusters were identified in London (Webber 1977a), and at the national scale for wards and parishes (Webber 1977c) and for local authorities (Imber 1977).

These studies increased awareness of the potential of composite social indicators for geographically defined populations for application in social policy and planning. For example, the work in Liverpool formed the basis of the Liverpool Social Malaise Exercise, and Imber's (1977) classification of local authorities was used by the DHSS to assist local authorities in assessing their position relative to others in the country. However, these social indicators were often weak in terms of their theoretical basis. They provided an efficient way to summarize the socio-economic profile of the population, but did not accurately reflect the characteristics of population need which were most relevant to welfare service objectives (Bebbington and Davies 1981).

These general area social indicators may be contrasted with the Resource Allocation Working Party (RAWP) formula for NHS resource allocation, which employs area statistics on mortality and demography, considered to be more direct measures of need for health care (DHSS 1975). The elements of the formula were therefore based on some concept of the type of need for which health care should be provided, and the factors which create variation in such need. It has been suggested that this method may not adequately take account of the complexity of social factors which influence local needs for care

)HSS 1986b). Although the RAWP proposed that the formula might
e applied to subregional, as well as regional, resource allocation, it
ay not adequately reflect the local differences in communities which
re relevant to need for resource spending. Also mortality rates may
ot be adequate surrogates for the health needs of the chronically ill
nd handicapped in an area.

Several alternative area indicators of need for health care have been
roposed, which include information about socio-economic deprivation
nd morbidity, as well as demography and mortality. Jarman (1983)
as put forward a weighted score of Census variables, the
'nder-Privileged Areas Score, which reflects the views of doctors
bout the factors likely to affect their workloads in deprived urban
reas. Thunhurst (1985) and Townsend, Phillimore, and Beattie (1988)
iscuss other indicators which include measures of morbidity as well
s mortality and social conditions. Several regional health authorities
se measures of socio-economic deprivation as criteria for subregional
:source allocation to districts.

These indicators are still rather crude approximations to need.
lthough their authors claim some theoretical or empirical basis for
ie selection of component variables, or the weightings attached to
iem, they are not fully validated as measures which are associated
ith population needs to which welfare services should be addressed.

The method employed for calculation of personal social service
eeds for the block grant represents a rather different use of area social
idicators (Bebbington and Davies 1980, 1982; Bebbington and Curtis
981). The method – although it is methodologically sophisticated and
:latively complex – has the advantage of overcoming two problems
a the application of social indicators to social planning. The first of
iese is that routinely collected socio-economic information available
or all parts of the country at a local scale suitable for planning is
)o general for calculation of precise welfare resource needs. On the
ther hand, detailed survey data on service needs of priority groups,
ollected in national social surveys, is based on geographically
ratified samples of respondents and does not provide representative
iformation about all localities in the country. The system described
ere enables a marriage of the two types of data to estimate relative
opulation needs.

For the elderly, and for children under 5 years, national sample
irvey data (Hunt 1978; Bone 1978) was used to identify 'target
roups' in the sample who were in need of particular types of social
:rvices. The survey data permitted need to be defined in terms of
:tailed information about respondents' circumstances. Also included
a the survey data were socio-economic indicators which corresponded
) information collected routinely in the Census. These socio-economic

129

indicators were used as 'predictors' in statistical formulae to calculate the probability of belonging to a target group. The 'predictor' equations could then be applied to Census data for local authorities throughout the country to predict the numbers of people in need of social services by 'synthetic estimation'.

This type of approach is also of interest because it enables the use of information about how lay people assess their circumstances as well as professional views about need. A number of survey methods are now available which enable us to collect systematic data on the way that people perceive their state of health and well-being, and their satisfaction with services provided and the services which they wish to receive. This sort of information must be interpreted with care since data on circumstances and needs reported by respondents are different from observed measurements using independent tests. However, reported measures of health are now quite widely used by the health and welfare services to complement other data sources, such a professional evaluations, Census data, and indicators of activities of welfare services (Curtis and Woods 1983; Hunt, McEwen, and McKenna 1987; Cartwright 1986; Jones, Leneman, and Maclean 1987). The relevance of lay views about need for planning welfare provision is considered in Chapter 8.

Fiscal pressure and central control in public welfare provision

The 1980s have seen a decline in the financial and political autonomy of local authorities, partly because of development of greater central government control and constraint on public sector spending and on patterns of local taxation. In some areas this is accompanied by a trend towards decentralization of responsibility for local expenditure and service provision to the neighbourhood level. Modification of the systems of territorial resource allocation have also been introduced over recent years to make spending correspond with relative population need, and this has resulted in some redistribution of resources, especially for the NHS. This redistribution, introduced under conditions of fiscal constraint, has necessitated greatest reductions in areas which have been considered to be historically over-resourced, typically those in the south and east of the country especially London.

However, these areas have experienced great difficulty in controlling their spending. Even in relatively well-provided areas, the use of health and welfare services is essentially constrained by the supply of care. Demand for services tends to expand to use available provision, and reduction of provision disappoints public expectations. The reductions in welfare provision, especially of hospital service

estrictions, have been unpopular developments. Particularly at the
ocal level, it has been politically and practically difficult to achieve
rational shifts in resources while maintaining satisfactory levels of
are. Nevertheless, the emphasis in welfare policy is very much on
ost limitation and the search for the most efficient way to provide
velfare services, whether through the public or private sector. As
central government pursues new ways of cutting the shrinking resource
ake, issues of territorial justice in public resource allocation have
ecome increasingly important.

Chapter eight

The geography of welfare needs and provision

The previous chapters have shown that certain vulnerable groups in the UK population have specific socio-geographical attributes which influence their welfare needs and their demand for, and use of, welfare services. As a result, different types of clients make varying and often conflicting demands on the welfare services, and especially in the present climate of fiscal stringency hard decisions about relative priorities have to be made. In certain parts of the UK, such as the inner cities where there are concentrations of vulnerable groups, the problems of making these decisions are particularly acute.

These issues have led to much discussion of what are the appropriate objectives for welfare provision. There is considerable variation in the pattern of welfare provision throughout the UK reflecting local differences in ideology, political culture, and welfare policy as much as population differences. It is difficult for central and local welfare agencies to decide which model of territorial justice is appropriate for welfare provision, and just as difficult to find effective ways of moving towards the objectives of service accessibility and uptake, or the still more elusive aims of greater equity in well-being for the members of society. This concluding chapter considers whether it is possible for welfare provision to be guided by fundamental principles defining need and social equity, and whether the inequalities in welfare provision described in the rest of the book imply social and inter-territorial inequity.

Physiological needs and basic rights

There are some types of welfare provision which can be identified as responses to basic physiological requirements for food, shelter, and protection from environmental hazard, which are essential to human functioning. According to Maslow's (1954) classification of needs these are the most fundamental needs, which must be met as a priority above other types of need. In the UK, as in most developed countries,

132

ther 'needs' are also considered as fundamental, although they are
ot physiological essentials, for example, the need for access to
rimary and secondary education. Rawls (1972), whose theory will be
iscussed in more detail, identified 'primary goods': 'things which a
ational man wants whatever else he wants ... rights, liberties,
pportunities and powers, income and wealth.' The United Nations
eclaration of Human Rights is perhaps the most widely accepted
nternational statement of the types of human needs which all people
hould be able to satisfy 'as of right'.

Part of the objective of public welfare provision in the UK is to
aintain minimum standards which ensure that these basic needs
sometimes termed 'merit goods') are met for everyone. On the face
f it, the minimum standard criterion may seem rather straightforward,
mplying that people should have automatic access to public provision
which will ensure that fundamental human requirements are met.
ervices like NHS care, and education from 5 to 16, for which all
re eligible, were partly inspired by this ideal.

However, distinctions are made between inadequate levels of
well-being and need for public welfare provision. For many services
which are provided to people individually, the public welfare system
ifferentiates between those whose needs should be met and others
or whom public provision will not be made, even for basic
hysiological needs. Meals are provided to the elderly and children
nly under certain conditions of incapacity or poverty. Housing
epartments distinguish between those who are intentionally homeless
nd those who are homeless through no action of their own. Some
atients, such as children, old age pensioners, and people with some
hronic illnesses receive free medicines and dental and ophthalmic
are through the NHS, other people have to pay for these services
ven when they are necessary.

Pre-school education is provided for some children, but not for
thers. These procedures leave significant numbers of people in the
JK for whom public welfare provision will not respond to even
undamental needs because they do not meet the eligibility criteria.
herefore, the public welfare system rations resources rather
tringently, even for maintenance of basic standards. The principles
or this rationing do not rest on a single criterion, but represent a
ombination of ideas about need and justice.

In practice, British social policy seems to represent a blend of
pproaches and criteria for assessing need and equity in welfare
rovision. One of the tensions in welfare policy is between the wish
n the one hand to provide welfare services universally, and on the
ther hand to concentrate public resources for welfare on those most
n need. The first requirement seems to be based on ideas about

133

fundamental needs and rights which society should provide for every
one, and the fact that providing services only for those who fall belov
minimum standards imparts a sense of social stigma to their use. A
the same time, there is a feeling that it is inappropriate to allocat
public resources to benefit those who are already relatively privilege

The framework and context of equity in welfare provision

Daniels (1987: ch. 9) suggests that when addressing questions c
public welfare, we need to bear in mind two aspects of the probler
at issue: the framework, and the context of compliance. Th
framework of analysis, in this case, describes the extent to which basi
social, economic, and political systems are considered to be fixed c
open to change. The context of compliance explains how far differer
parts of the framework comply with the principles of social justic
that we wish to promote. Rawls's (1972) contractual theory of socia
justice assumed that the basic institutions would comply wit
principles of social justice. It is difficult to apply principles of socia
justice meaningfully to more superficial parts of the welfare syster
if the basic institutions cannot be assumed to comply with thes
principles. This framework and context approach leads us to consider
first, whether there are inequities in the structure of our basi
institutions, and second, what is the significance of inequalities in les
fundamental aspects of the welfare system. This book has bee
particularly concerned with the extent to which geographical factor
contribute to, or reflect, such inequities.

Marxist structuralist interpretations

A Marxist interpretation would suggest that the capitalis
socio-economic structure is fundamentally inequitable. Radical socia
theory stresses basic human needs as inalienable rights, and writer
using structuralist theories have explained the activities of the welfar
state in providing education, housing, and health care as a respons
to the requirements of the capitalist society for reproduction of labou
power and stability in the socio-political system. Harvey's (1973
account of cities in countries like Britain explains urban geograph
as driven by the requirements of industrial capitalism and woul
interpret many of the geographical variations in space observed in thi
book as arising from these structural forces, which create space b
deploying fixed capital assets, create and maintain demand fo
industrial products, and circulate surplus value. Marxist theor
postulates social processes at work which will ultimately change thi

fundamental structure (Pinch 1985: ch. 5; Jones and Moon 1987: 349–61; Deacon 1984; Navarro 1976, 1980).

These structural interpretations emphasize the significance of social reproduction and the need to create goods and services to ensure the survival of society as a whole. Here we have largely been concerned with the implication of variations in the real income and well-being of individuals. Marxists might argue that the socialist mode of production would ensure a just distribution of individual welfare, which would also be optimal for society as a whole. Marxist theory brings together ideas of production and distribution of goods and services in society (Harvey 1978: 15). Its greatest strength as a means of analysis is that it shows clearly how, in capitalist societies, structural factors are responsible for generating some of the inequalities observed here.

Liberal interpretations

However, in spite of the power of Marxist and neo-Marxist analyses, the framework of welfare in Britain today shows us that industrial capitalism is viewed as a fixed aspect of our society, and that the sort of changes anticipated by Marxist theory are not desirable to most people in this country. Certainly, current trends seem to indicate that our society is moving further away from socialist goals, although not all its members are content with the direction in which we are moving. The capitalist system is often justified on the ground that all members of society have equal opportunity to express their views through the democratic political system; and a liberal system fosters healthy competition, on terms of equal opportunity, for access to different positions in society. According to this interpretation, inequalities arise because of the natural differences between individuals and the exercise of individual free choice.

Libertarian theories are based on the view that it is essential to retain self-determination for individuals, and that it is socially and economically damaging to impose too great a degree of uniformity and equality on the members of society. The degree of equality in welfare provision required by these libertarian theories is not great. Hayek (1973) argues that it is not realistic for government to aim for equality of opportunity (except in a very limited sense, with respect to aspects such as access to public office), because to do so government 'would have to control the whole physical and human environment of all persons' (p.84). The more limited definition of justice proposed by Hayek is a situation which accords with the constraints which public institutions and joint activities must satisfy if persons engaging in them are to have no complaints against them.

135

Hayek's views seem to be concordant with those of the present Conservative policy-makers in Britain.

The libertarian view implies that the basic institutional frameworks with which we should be concerned are the pathways into political and administrative positions, which carry influence over social policies and practices, and into occupations with varying levels of remuneration. This book has considered the socio-geographical constraints on these fundamental aspects of equality of opportunity. The jurisdictional partitioning of space affects the way in which communities may influence basic political processes, and evidence discussed in Chapters 3 and 7 shows that the question of central–local government relations and of the existence of regional levels of administration are crucial in this respect.

We have also seen that certain sectors of society, such as ethnic minorities, which have a very uneven and locally concentrated distribution in space, are under-represented in senior positions in institutions such as Parliament, local authorities, schools, and the health service. This is a legitimate source of complaint against basic political and administrative institutions, and even liberal philosophers such as Hayek would presumably consider the situation unjust. These are among the most basic inequities in the British framework, which need to be rectified.

The indicators we might apply to assess equity at this basic level should relate to the extent of representation of particular communities in the essential institutions such as central and local government and bureaucracies. Although some would condemn as discriminatory exercises such as racial monitoring of employees in local government and the civil service, they are necessary to assess the likely inequities in representation of underprivileged minorities, especially in those parts of the country where they are concentrated. The role of agencies, such as the Equal Opportunities Commission and the Commission for Racial Equality, are important in so far as they can help to ensure social justice in the basic institutions of the United Kingdom.

Contractarian theory is more optimistic about the possibility of defining social justice on philosophical grounds, based on the principle of fairness in the distribution of social resources. Rawls (1972) has proposed the contractual theory of social justice, which defines the pattern of distribution of social resources which would be the outcome of a 'contract' between the members of society made under hypothetical circumstances (the 'original position') in which no one knew his or her position in the socio-economic structure. Rawls's theory requires that resources be distributed in such a way that the least disadvantaged members of society are not made worse off. This social responsibility applies to 'primary social goods' such as basic liberties; freedom of movement; choice of occupation; powers of office, income, and wealth; and social bases of self-respect.

Some writers have extended this philosophical stance to argue for social policies which would seek to achieve greater equality in the distribution of society's resources. Le Grand (1982: ch. 8) argues that greater equality is not necessarily prejudicial to diversity. He distinguishes between those aspects of the pattern of resource distribution which reflect individual choices and those which do not. Society is deemed to have a responsibility to ensure that when the distribution of welfare services is not wholly determined by individual choice, then such distribution is fair. Le Grand argues for a more equal distribution of income as a more effective method to achieve equality than the provision of welfare services. This approach suggests that our most powerful indicators of territorial equity are those which tell us about the geographical variation in income. However, policies for income redistribution should take account of the fact that many of those most in need of many of the welfare services that we have considered in this book are not those who directly dispose of income. They include, for example, children and women who may have little control over the household budget (Pahl 1980, 1985). For this reason, welfare payments such as child benefit are particularly important as means of supporting low income families.

Some writers have considered the applications of philosophical theories of social justice to the distribution of public welfare services. Daniels (1987) has extended Rawls's arguments in the context of health care. He argues that health care is a special case, but his conclusions are relevant to some local authority services as well as the health service. Daniels starts with the premiss that a suitable criterion for whose needs should be met by public provision is that public provision should maximize the chances that all members of society have the normal opportunity range. Health care should be provided to ensure that all people can achieve the normal opportunity range in so far as modern medicine makes this possible. Similar arguments might be applied to access to education which affects achievement and life opportunities. This theory of a socially just distribution implies that services should be provided to those who do not have access to the normal opportunity range. Only those services which restore, wholly or partly, the normal range of functions and opportunity would be provided. According to this argument, other aspects of service provision, which cannot be shown to influence this outcome, should not be the concern of public services. This formulation of social justice implies that the most relevant criteria for allocation of health care resources relate to functional disability and handicap and the impact of services in reducing the effects of disability.

In the context of health care, it has also been argued that social justice should correspond to equality of access opportunity to welfare services. Aday, Anderson, and Fleming (1980) have proposed that the pattern of provision should ensure that the pattern of use of services corresponds to need. Differences in access to services which do not influence utilization patterns are accepted, even though they may mean that the cost of the services is greater for some consumers (in terms of time, money, or effort) than for others. An alternative view might be that individuals with similar needs should have equal access opportunity to services, even if this does not relate to their utilization behaviour. This interpretation does not allow any differences in the cost of obtaining care between individuals (Sloan, and Bentkover 1979). The operational outcome of either of these formulations of social justice would, of course, depend on the criterion of need that is used (Daniels 1987).

Professional and lay views of welfare needs

The arguments considered so far suggest that most welfare services should be provided by the public sector for at least two reasons. First, because the more basic social institutions fail to comply fully with the requirements of liberal arguments of social justice. Welfare provision therefore needs to be targeted towards those whose social or geographical position makes them so disadvantaged by inequities in the socio-economic system that they are unable to bear the cost of obtaining welfare services which they need. Second, those in favour of public sector provision argue that even for more privileged people and geographical areas, the commercial sector is not cost-effective at providing the required range and quality of welfare services. If public services are aiming to compensate deprived groups for inequities in access to welfare services, and also to compensate for imperfections in the market as a provider of welfare services, they must operate on some definition of the type of client who needs to use a particular type of service.

Economic criteria might be used as a basis for assessing need, and at the beginning of this book we have considered some concepts from welfare economics which help to assess patterns of welfare provision. The guiding economic principle is to maximize the benefits for individual consumers and society as a whole derived from the inputs made through welfare provision. However, the arguments from welfare economics are difficult to apply to welfare provision because it is hard to assess and compare the costs and benefits which arise from consumption of welfare. If a valid basis can be found to measure inputs and outputs (the latter being particularly difficult), welfare economics may provide a rigorous paradigm for assessing the outcomes of different types of welfare provision, and the type of provision which will most effectively produce the desired outcome for a particular client. The Audit Commission's (1987a) report explains how the 'value for money' approach can be applied to the evaluation of care of clients, such as the elderly, in order to decide what type of care should be provided to which clients.

Knapp (1984) has pointed out that much work in welfare economics relates to intermediate outputs (such as services provided) rather than final outputs (such as changes in welfare). Economics tells us little about how to assess or compare essentially qualitative outcomes, although ideas such as 'quality of life years' have been used for this purpose. How do we evaluate improved education for a child against benefits for an elderly person receiving domiciliary care? Economic definitions do not tell us how to set the aims of welfare provision in terms of the welfare outcomes desired. These decisions must rest on the judgements of professional and lay people about the benefits which we should expect from welfare provision.

The allocation of resources to individuals and areas rests partly on expert opinion about the type of provision which should be made. For example, opinions about the cause of inadequate welfare and the type of provision which may be effective in improving welfare. This is particularly true of medical service provision which depends to a large extent on clinical judgements about the type of care and treatment patients should receive. Social workers and teachers are other examples of professionals whose opinions are likely to be sought to assess the welfare needs of the population in an area. However, professional opinion is often not unanimous about the needs which should be met – e.g. the recent controversy over children taken into care in Cleveland because of diagnosed sexual abuse considered in the Butler-Sloss report on cases in Cleveland (Cambell 1988; GB. Parliament 1988).

In some cases, the government seeks to impose a particular response to need regardless of the views of individual professionals; for example, the list of medicines from which doctors may prescribe under the NHS is defined by the government. The new Education Reform Act seeks to impose uniformity on the school curriculum, and therefore weakens the individual teacher's control over what are defined as pupils' educational needs. Thus welfare provision is not entirely governed by the views of experts who administer care.

To some extent, non-expert, lay opinions about need are also taken into account, These are the views of consumers, and potential consumers, who make demands for services, or desire services. This type of need has been characterized by Bradshaw (1972) as 'expressed' or 'felt' need. These may be distinguished from

139

'normative' or 'comparative' needs, which correspond more to professional views about welfare provision. Also to some extent, it might be argued that the democratic process allows expression of lay views. Survey methodology and ethnographic techniques can be used to reveal lay views of need, assessed by the measures of reported well-being discussed in Chapter 7. The examples discussed in this book show that the felt and expressed needs of different groups in society are variable (e.g. between different ethnic groups). Current trends towards greater public participation in welfare service planning and to more emphasis consumer satisfaction, tend to give more weight to these types of need.

Many writers have pointed to the difficulty of basing welfare provision on expressed wants of consumers (Fitzgerald 1977). One problem is that some felt needs would not justify welfare provision in the eyes of others. Another strong argument against this interpretation of need is the degree to which wants are constrained by limited and inaccurate perceptions of available services and of the form of provision most likely to meet felt needs. We cannot assume that consumers would choose welfare services on the basis of perfect or specialist knowledge.

However, these criticisms of a more consumer-oriented approach to assessment of need have ignored its greatest merit, that it tends to avoid the limitations of thinking of need in terms of what welfare services currently provide. Lay people's perceptions are more likely than those of professionals to indicate forms of welfare delivery which will seem appropriate and acceptable to the client. They are also relevant to preventative interventions and those intended to promote individual behaviour beneficial to well-being. Lay views of welfare needs may be rather conservative – for example, people often seem more willing to defend acute hospital services than community health care. However, the view from the community may show that there are dimensions of well-being to which welfare provision is not directed. Chapters 4–6 in this book have attempted to demonstrate the more holistic view which is obtained by examining the position of vulnerable groups as types of people needing a range of welfare services rather than as clients for a particular service considered in isolation. There does seem to be a case for developing procedures for planning of welfare provision which will take into account lay views of need and the value of different welfare outcomes.

Priority areas for positive discrimination: contributions of welfare geography

It has been argued here that while liberal theories of social justice accept as given a system which will create inequalities, they require, at the same time, equality in basic social institutions, and also in some interpretations equality of opportunity. This book presents evidence that the basic institutions do not operate equitably, and this implies a need for positive discrimination in favour of the worst-off members of society.

The implementation of positive discrimination policies has, in many cases, relied on area-based programmes, and the use of social indicators for geographically defined populations. Thus ideas about individual disadvantage have been translated into the concept of deprived areas requiring positive discrimination. The Urban Programme, the Educational Priority Areas, and Housing Action Areas are examples which have been considered in preceding chapters; the history of these schemes, discussed earlier, raises interesting questions about how far an ecological approach to positive discrimination is appropriate, and which are the salient social indicators for classification of priority areas.

It is not clear, for example, whether territorial needs are simply the sum of the individual needs of the population in the area (Bennett 1980: 91). In some cases, there are attributes of the locality itself which influence needs for welfare resources, and the concentration of vulnerable groups in some deprived areas may tend to produce a multiplicative effect of deprivation. Area-based policies have also been criticized for failing to direct resources effectively to those who are most in need. Experience to date suggests that while geographical areas with high concentrations of vulnerable groups may provide a suitable focus for welfare policies, the welfare provision within these zones must be carefully designed to reach the target groups for which the services are intended.

If area-based planning is to be more effective, the assessment of local need and suitable welfare responses should be improved. What is required is a better understanding of the processes which produce deprivation and affect access to welfare services in these priority areas. This can be partly informed by a better appreciation by policy-makers and the public of the political and bureaucratic processes which govern the present socio-economic inequalities and welfare service provision. This text has made several references to authors who have reviewed explanations of these processes (e.g. Pinch 1985; Bennett 1980). The more qualitative and ethnographic studies of vulnerable groups also have an important contribution to make in raising awareness of the factors which shape lay people's behaviour and choices which influence the appropriateness and accessibility of services for them (e.g. Cornwell 1984; Donovan 1986). The new emphasis on locality planning and involvement of the community through public participation may facilitate the provision of services well adapted to the needs of local people, and it can usefully draw on ideas from social geography about what distinguishes communities and how they function (e.g. Bell and Newby 1972).

The future for the geography of public welfare provision

This book has argued that a large number of processes, some of them intrinsically geographical, create inequalities and inequities in the pattern of well-being and the ways in which public welfare is provided. In British society, as in many western capitalist nations, we are still far from ensuring social and geographical equity in opportunity for well-being; and for this reason, we should continue to concern ourselves with the social and spatial distribution of needs and the extent to which these are met through the welfare services.

According to many observers, we are witnessing the public welfare system in a state of crisis as it is eroded by government policies which favour the transfer of welfare provision to the private or voluntary sector. Those supporting this trend away from public welfare provision argue that the change will provide services which are more efficient and responsive to clients' requirements. However, this text has also reviewed evidence that the growth of the private sector has significant geographical dimensions, which are developing in ways which will be detrimental to models of welfare provision which stress equality and equity of access to services.

While in the UK the role of local authorities and the NHS in public welfare provision may be declining, they seem likely to retain some role in the management of welfare provision, even though this may be done through contractual arrangements with providers in the private or voluntary sector. The discussion in this chapter suggests that even in a libertarian system, which accepts some inequality in consumption of welfare, it is detrimential to equity to allow all control over the consumption of welfare services to be left to 'market forces'. All societies should continue to strive for social justice in the distribution of welfare and opportunities between their members. Whether or not the public sector adopts a more minor part in the provision of services, the demographic, social, and geographical factors which determine varying need for welfare services will continue to be of public concern.

References

Abler, R., Adams, J., and Gould, P. (1971) *Spatial Organisation*, Englewood Cliffs, NJ: Prentice-Hall.

Aday, L., Anderson, L., and Fleming, G. (1980) *Health Care in the US: Equitable for Whom?*, Beverly Hills, Calif.: Sage.

Advisory Council on Child Care (1974) *Care and Treatment in a Planned Environment*, London: HMSO.

Ahmed, S. (1984) '"Second generation immigrant" is a complete distortion of English', *Social Work Today* 16: 12–13.

Aiach, P., Carr-Hill, R., Curtis, S., and Illesley, R. (1988) *Les Inégalites Sociales de Santé en France et en Grande-Bretagne: analyse et étude Comparative*, Paris: INSERM/Documentation Française.

Anderson, T. and Egland, J. (1961) 'Spatial aspects of social area analysis', *American Sociological Review* 26: 392–8.

Arnold, E. (1982) 'Finding black families for black children in Britain', in J. Cheetham (ed.) *Social Work and Ethnicity*, London: Allen & Unwin, pp. 98–111.

Ashton, P. (1984) 'Poverty and the beholder', *New Society*, 18 October, pp. 95–8.

Association of Directors of Social Services and the Commission for Racial Equality (1978) *Multi-Racial Britain: The Social Services' Response*, London: CRE.

Association of District Councils, Association of London Authorities, Association of Metropolitan Authorities, and London Boroughs Association (1986) *The Local Case for Housing*, London: AMA.

Atkinson, A., Maynard, A., Trinder, C. (1983) *Parents and Children: Incomes in Two Generations*, London: Heinemann Educational Books.

Audit Commission (1984) *Obtaining Better Value in Education: Aspects of Non-Teaching Costs in Secondary Education*, London: HMSO.

Audit Commission (1987a) *Making a Reality of Community Care*, London: HMSO.

Audit Commission (1987b) *The Management of London's Authorities: Preventing the Breakdown of Services*, London: HMSO.

Babbage, A. (1973) 'House improvement in stress areas', *Environmental Health* 81: 278–82.

Bagley, C., Bart, M., and Wong, J. (1979) 'Antecedents of scholastic

143

success in West Indian ten year olds in London', in G. Verma and C. Baley (eds) *Race Education and Identity*, London: Macmillan.

Balchin, P. (1979) *Housing Improvement and Social Inequality*, Farnborough: Saxon House.

Balchin, P. (1985) *Housing Policy: An Introduction*, London: Croom Helm.

Bandaranayke, R. (1986) 'Ethnic difference in disease – an epidemiological perspective', in T. Rathwell and D. Phillips (eds) *Health, Race and Ethnicity*, London: Croom Helm, ch. 3.

Barnard, K. (1982) 'Retirement housing in the UK: a geographical appraisal', in A. Warnes (ed.) *Geographical Perspectives on the Elderly*, London: Wiley, ch. 7.

Barnes, J., and Lucas, H. (1974) 'Positive discrimination in education: individuals, groups and institutions', in T. Leggatt (ed.) *Sociology Theory and Socical Research*, London: Sage.

Bassett, K. and Short, J.(1980) *Housing and Residential Structure: Alternative Approaches*, London: Routledge & Kegan Paul.

Bebbington, A. and Curtis, S. (1981) *Territorial Variations in State Provided Day Care Services for Children under 5*, Discussion Paper 220, Personal Social Services Research Unit, University of Kent.

Bebbington, A. and Davies, D. (1980), 'Territorial need indicators. A new approach: the intellectual context', *Journal of Social Policy* 9(2): 145–68.

Bebbington, A. and Davies, D. (1981) 'Territorial need indicators. A new approach: II, the personal social services for the elderly', *Journal of Social Policy* 9(4): 33–62.

Bebbington, A. and Davies, B. (1982) 'Patterns of social service provision for the elderly', in A. Warnes (ed.) *Geographical Perspectives on the Elderly*, London: Wiley, pp. 355–74.

Bebbington, A., Davies, B., Charnley, H., Ferlie, E., Hughes, M., and Twigg, J. (1988) *Resources, Needs and Outcomes in Community Care*, Aldershot: Gower.

Bell, C., and Newby, H. (1972) *Community Studies: An Introduction to the Sociology of the Local Community*, London: George Allen and Unwin.

Bennett, R. (1980) *The Geography of Public Finance: Welfare under Discal Federalism and Local Government finance*, London: Methuen.

Bennett, R. (1982) *Central Grants to Local Government*, Cambridge, Cambridge University Press.

Bevan, G., Copeman, H., Perrin, J., and Rosser, R. (1980) *Health Care Priorities and Management*, London: Croom Helm.

Bevan, G. and Mays, N. (1987) *Resource Allocation in the Health Service: A Review of the Methods of the Resource Allocation Working Party*, London: Routledge & Kegan Paul.

Beveridge, W. (1942) Social Insurance and Allied Services, London: HMSC

Blaxter, M. (1981) *The Health of the Children*, London: Croom Helm.

Bone, M. (1978) *Preschool Children and the Need for Day Care*, London OPCS/HMSO.

Booth, C. (1892) *The Life and Labour of the People of London*, Vol. II, London: Macmillan.

Bosanquet, N. (1982) 'Patients or doctors first?', *New Society*, 31 July, p. 220.

Bourne, L. (1981) *The Geography of Housing*, London: Edward Arnold.

Bowlby, J. (1956) *Child Care and the Growth of Love*, Harmondsworth: Penguin.

Bradshaw, J. (1972) 'The concept of social need', *New Society*, 30 March, pp. 640–3.

Bramley, G. (1979) 'The inner city labour market', in C. Jones (ed.) *Urban Deprivation and the Inner City*, London: Croom Helm, pp.63–91.

Briggs, A. (1961) *Social Thought and Social Action: A Study of the Work of Seebohm Rowntree 1871–1954*, London: Longman.

British Medical Journal (1979) 'Rickets in Asian immigrants, vol. 1, 6180', *British Medical Journal*, 30 July, p.1744.

Brown, C. (1984) *Black and White in Britain*, London: Policy Studies Institute, reprinted in 1985.

Bruner, J. (1980) *Under Five in Britain*, London: Grant McIntyre.

Bryne, T. (1983) *The Local Government System*, Harmondsworth: Penguin.

Bryne, T. and Padfield, C. (1985) *Social Services Made Simple*, London: Heinemann.

Buchanon, J. (1968) *The Demand and Supply of Public Goods,* Chicago: Rand McNally.

Burgess, T. and Travers, T. (1980) *Ten Billion Pounds: Whitehall's Takeover of the Town Halls*, London: Grant McIntyre.

Cambell, B. (1988) *Unofficial Secrets: Child Abuse – the Cleveland Case*, London: Virago.

Carter, H. (1972) *The Study of Urban Geography*, London: Edward Arnold.

Cartwright, A. (1986) *Health Surveys in Practice and Potential*, London: King's Fund.

Central Advisory Council for Education (1963) *Half Our Future. Report of Central Advisory Council for Education* (Chairman, Sir John Newson), Department of Education and Science, London: HMSO.

Central Advisory Council for Education (1967) *Children and their Primary Schools. Report of the Central Advisory Council for Education (England)* (Chair, Lady Plowden), Department of Education and Science, London: HMSO.

Central Housing Advisory Committee (1961) *Homes for Today and Tomorrow. Report of a Sub-Committee of the Central Housing Advisory Committee*, Department of the Environment, London: HMSO.

Central Statistical Office CSO (1983) *Social Trends 1983*, London: HMSO.

CSO) (1986) *Social Trends 1986*, London: HMSO.

CSO (1987) *Regional Trends 22*, London: HMSO.

Chadwick, E. (1842) *Report from the Poor Law Commissioners on an Inquiry on the Sanitary Condition of the Labouring Population of Great Britain*, London: HMSO, reprinted, 1965.

References

Charlton, W., Rawstron, E., Rees, F. (1979) 'Regional disparities at A-level', *Geography* 64(1): 26–36.

Cheetham, J. (ed.) (1982) *Social Work and Ethnicity*, London: Allen & Unwin.

Chilvers, C. (1978) 'Regional mortality, 1969–1973', *Population Trends* 11: 16–20.

Chisholm, M. (1975) *Reformation of Local Government in England*, London.

Clarke, G. (1982) *Housing and Planning in the Countryside*, Chichester: Research Studies Press.

Clarke, M. and Clayton, D. (1983) 'The quality of obstetric care provided for Asian immigrants in Leicestershire, *British Medical Journal*, 19 February, p.261.

Clarke, M. and Wilson, A. (1987) 'Developments in planning models for health care policy analysis', in M. Pacione (ed.) *Medical Geography in Progress and Prospect*, London: Croom Helm, pp. 248–76.

Coleman, A. (1985) *Utopia on Trial*, London: Hilary Shipman.

Commission for Racial Equality (CRE) (1983) *Ethnic Minority Hospital Staff,* London: CRE.

CRE (1984a) *Hackney Housing Investigated: Summary of a Formal Investigation,* London: CRE.

CRE (1984b) *Race and Council Housing in Hackney: Report of a Formal Investigation,* London: CRE.

Community Relations Commission (CRC) (1975) *Who Minds? A Study of Working Mothers and Child Minding in Ethnic Minority Communities,* London: CRC.

Comptroller and Auditor-General (1984) *The Housing Benefits Scheme. Report by the Comptroller and Auditor-General*, London: HMSO.

Cooper, S. (1981) *Rural Poverty in the United Kingdom*, London: Policy Studies Institute.

Cornwell, J. (1984) *Hard Earned Lives: Accounts of Health and Illness from East London*, London: Tavistock.

Creighton, S. (1980) *Child Victims of Physical Abuse 1976. Third Report on Findings of the NSPCC Special Units Registers*, London: NSPCC.

Cullingford *et al.* (1975) *Liverpool Social Area Analysis (Interim Report)*, Planning Research Applications Group.

Cullingford, S. and Openshaw, N. (1979) *Deprived Places or Deprived People?* Discussion Paper 20, Centre for Urban and Regional Development Studies, Newcastle.

Culyer, A., Lavers, R., and Williams, A. (1972) 'Health Indicators', in A. Schonfield and S. Shaw (eds) *Social Indicators and Social Policy*, London: Heinemann.

Curtis, S. (1980) 'Spatial access, need and equity: an analysis of the accessibility of primary health facilities for the elderly in parts of East Kent. Vols I and II', unpublished D.Phil. thesis, University of Kent.

Curtis, S. (1983) *Intra-Urban Variations in Health and Health Care. Research Report*, Queen Mary College, University of London.

Curtis, S. and Ogden, P. (1987) 'Bangladeshis in London: a challenge to welfare', *Revue Européenne des Migrations Internationales* 2(3) 135–49.

Curtis, S. and Woods, K. (1983) 'Health care in London: planning issues and the ocntribution of local morbidity surveys', in M. Clarke (ed.) *Planning and analysis in Health Care Systems*, London Papers in Regional Science No. 13, London: Pion, pp. 57–77

Dahl, R. (1956) *A Preface to Democratic Theory*, Chicago: University of Chicago Press.

Daniels, N. (1987) *Just Health Care*, London: Cambridge University Press.

Darton, R. (1984) 'Trends 1970–81', in Laming et al. (eds) *Residential Care for the Elderly: Present Problems and Future Issues*, Discussion Paper No. 8, Policy Studies Institute, London.

Davie, R., Butler, N., and Goldstein, H., (1972) *From Birth to Seven: The Second Report of the National Child Development Study (1958 Cohort)*, London: Longman.

Davies, B. (1968) *Social Needs and Resources in Local Services*, London: Michael Joseph.

Davies, B., Barton, A., and McMillan, I. (1971) *Variations in Children's Services among British Urban Authorities*, London: Bell.

Davies, B., Barton, A., McMillan, I., and Williamson, K. (1971) *Variations in Services for the Elderly*, London: Bell.

Deacon, B. (1984) 'Medical care and health under state socialism', *International Journal of Health Services* 14: 453–80.

Dean, C. (1983) 'Winners and losers in the recent coaching revolution', *Area* 15(1): 1–6.

Department of Education and Science (DES) (1972) *Education: A Framework for Expansion*, London: HMSO.

DES (1977) *A New Partnership for Our Schools* (Taylor Committee), HMSO: DES.

Department of Environment (DoE) (1977) *Housing Policy: A Consultative Document*, London: HMSO.

DoE (1978) *National Dwelling and Housing Survey Report*, London: HMSO.

DoE (1985) *An Inquiry into the Conditions of the Local Authority Housing Stock in England, 1985*, London: HMSO.

Department of Health and Social Security (DHSS) (1968) *National Health Services. The Administrative Stucture of Medical and Related Services in England and Wales*, London: HMSO.

DHSS (1970) *The Future Structure of the National Health Service*, London: HMSO.

DHSS (1975) *Sharing Resources for Health in England and Wales*, London: HMSO.

DHSS (1981) *Community Care*, London: HMSO.

DHSS (1986a) *Neighbourhood Nursing: A Focus for Care* (DHSS), London: HMSO.

DHSS (1986b) *Review of the Resource Allocation Working Party Formula: Interim Report*, London: DHSS.

Department of Transport (DoT) (1977) *Local Transport Note 1/77: Survey of Concessionary Bus Fares for the Elderly and Disabled in England and Wales*, London: DoT.

147

References

DoT (1978) *Consultative Document on Transport Policy*, London: HMSO.

DoT (1979) *The National Travel Survey 1978/9*, London: DOT.

Dexter, M. and Harbert, W. (1983) *The Home Help Service*, London: Tavistock.

Donovan, J. (1983) 'Black people's health: a different way forward?', *Radical Community Medicine*, Vol. 6, Winter, 20–9.

Donovan, J. (1984) 'Ethnicity and health: a research review', *Social Science and Medicine* 19(7): 663–70.

Donovan, J. (1986) *'We Don't Buy Sickness, It Just Comes': Health, Illness and Health Care in the Lives of Black People in London*, Aldershot: Gower.

Douglas, J. and Bloomfield, J. (1958) *Children under Five. The Results of a National Survey Made by a Joint Committee of the Institute of Child Health*, Society of Medical Officers of Health and the Population Investigation Committee, London: Allen & Unwin.

Douglas, J. and Waller, R. (1966) 'Air pollution and respiratory infection of children', *British Journal of Preventative Medicine* 20(1): 1–8.

Duncan, S. (1976) 'Housing opportunities and constraints', *Transactions of the Institute of British Geographers* 1: 10–19.

Eggleston, S., Dunn, D., Anjali, M. (1986) *Education for Some*, London: Trentham Books.

English, J. (1979) 'Access and deprivation in local authority housing', in C. Jones (ed.) *Urban Deprivation and the Inner City*, London: Croom Helm, pp. 113–35.

Equal Opportunities Commission (1982) *Who Cares for the Carers? Opportunities for those Caring for the Elderly and Handicapped*, London: EOC.

Evans, M. (1983) 'Introduction', in M. Evans and C. Ungerson (eds) *Sexual Divisions*, London: Tavistock, pp. 1–14.

Eyles, J. and Woods, K. (1983) *The Social Geography of Medicine and Health*, London: Croom Helm.

Farrington, J. (1985) 'Transport geography and policy: deregulation and privatisation', *Transactions of the Institute of British Geographers* (n.s.), 10: 109–19.

Ferri, E. and Niblett, R. (1977) *Disadvantaged Families and Playgroups*, London: National Children's Bureau/NFER.

Fevre, R. (1984) *Cheap Labour and Racial Discrimination*, Aldershot: Gower.

Field, S., Hair, G., Rees, T., and Stevens, P. (1981) *Ethnic Minorities in Britain: A Study of Trends in the Position since 1961*, London: HMSO.

Finch, J. 1984 'The deceipt of self help', London: *Journal of Social Policy* 13: 1–20.

Finer, (1952) *Life and Times of Edwin Chadwick*, London: Methuen.

Fitzgerald, R. (1977) *Human Needs and Politics*, Oxford: Pergarron.

Forrest, R. (1982) 'The social implications of council house sales', in J. English (ed.) *The Future of Council Housing*, London: Croom Helm, pp. 97–114.

Forrest, R. and Murie, A. (1982) 'The great divide', *Roof*, November–December, pp. 19–21.

Forrest, R. and Murie, A. (1988) *Selling the Welfare State: The Privatisation of Public Housing*, London: Routledge.

Fox, A. and Adelstein, A. (1978) 'Occupational mortality: work or way of life?', *Journal of Epidemiology and Community Health* 36: 938–45.

Fox, A. and Goldblatt, P. (1982) 'Socio-demographic differences in mortality', *Population Trends* 27: pp. 8–13.

Fox, A., Jones, D., and Goldblatt, P. (1984) 'Approaches to studying the effect of socio-economic circumstances on geographic differences in mortality in England and Wales', *British Medical Bulletin* 40: 309–14.

Fraser, D. (1973) *The Evolution of the British Welfare State*, London: Macmillan.

Fryer, P. (1987) 'Oxford's aim of health for all', *Health Service Journal*, 5 March, pp. 274–75.

Gifford, Lord, QC (1986) *The Broadwater Farm Inquiry. Report of the Independent Inquiry into Disturbances of October 1985 at the Broadwater Farm Estate, Tottenham, Chaired by Lord Gifford QC*, London: Karia Press.

Gill, O. and Jackson, B. (1981) *Adoption and Race: Black, Asian and Mixed Race Children in Black Families*, London: Batsford.

Glaister, S. (1985) 'Competition on an urban bus route', *Journal of Transport, Economics and Policy* XIX(1): 65–82.

Glendenning, F. (1982) *Ethnic Minority Elderly People: Some Issues of Social Policy*, in Cheetham, J., *Social Work and Ethnicity*, London: Allen & Unwin, pp.122–32.

Gold, J. (1980) *Introduction to Behavioural Geography*, Oxford: Oxford University Press.

Gray, J. (1978) *School Reform and Educational Disadvantage*, Open University E361 Block 3, Unit 7, Milton Keynes: Open University Press.

Gray, J. and Jesson, D. (1987) *Education and Training, UK, 1987. Research Report*, The Old Vicarage, Hermitage.

Great Britain. Parliament (1961) *Royal Commission on Local Government in Greater London*, London: HMSO.

Great Britain. Parliament (1968a) *Report of the Committee on Local Authority and Allied Personal Social Services* (Chairman, F. Seebohm), Cmnd 3703, London: HMSO.

Great Britain. Parliament (1968b) *Old Houses into New Homes*, Cmnd 3602, London: HMSO.

Great Britain. Parliament (1969a) *Royal Commission on Local Government in England* (Chairman, Lord Redcliff-Maude), Cmnd 4040, London: HMSO.

Great Britain. Parliament (1969b) *Royal Commission of Local Government in England: Memorandum of Dissent by D. Senior, 1969*, Cmnd 4040-1, London: HMSO.

Great Britain. Parliament (1969c) *Local Government Reform. Short Version of the Royal Commission of Local Government in England*, Cmnd 4039, London: HMSO

Great Britain. Parliament (1972) *Education: A Framework for Expansion*, Cmnd 5174, London: HMSO.

Great Britain. Parliament (1974) *Report of the Committee on One Parent Families*, Cmnd 5629, London: HMSO.

Great Britain. Parliament (1975) *Race Relations and Housing*, Cmnd 6232, London: HMSO.

Great Britain. Parliament (1976a) *Fit for the Future: Report of the Select Committee on Child Health Services*, Cmnd 6684, London: HMSO.

Great Britain. Parliament (1976b) *Report of the Committee of Enquiry into Local Government Finance*, Cmnd 6453, London: HMSO.

Great Britain. Parliament (1979a) *Royal Commission on the Distribution of Income and Wealth, Report*, Cmnd 7615, London: HMSO.

Great Britain. Parliament (1979b) *Royal Commission on the National Health Service* (Chairman, Sir Alec Merrison), Cmnd 7615, London: HMSO.

Great Britain. Parliament (1979c) *Concessionary Fares for Elderly, Blind and Disabled People*, Cmnd 7475, London: HMSO.

Great Britain. Parliament (1981a) *The Brixton Disorders, April 10–12 1981. Report of an Enquiry*, Cmnd 8427, London: HMSO.

Great Britain. Parliament (1981b) *West Indian Children in Our Schools. Interim Report of the Committee of Inquiry into the Education of Children from Ethnic Minority Groups*, Cmnd 8273, London: HMSO.

Great Britain. Parliament (1981c) *Alternatives to Domestic Rates*, Cmnd 8449, London: HMSO.

Great Britain. Parliament (1981d) *Growing Older*, Cmnd 8172, London: HMSO.

Great Britain. Parliament (1983a) *Streamlining the Cities*, Cmnd 9063, London: HMSO.

Great Britain. Parliament (1983b) *Rates*, Cmnd 9008, London: HMSO.

Great Britain. Parliament (1984) *Buses*, Cmnd 9300, London: HMSO.

Great Britain. Parliament (1985a) *Housing Benefit. Report of the Review Team*, Cmnd 9520, London: HMSO.

Great Britain. Parliament (1985b) *Education for All*, Cmnd 9453, London: HMSO.

Great Britain. Parliament (1986) *Paying for Local Government*, Cmnd 9714, London HMSO.

Great Britain. Parliament (1987a) *Promoting Better Health: The Government's Programme for Improving Primary Health Care*, Cmnd. 249, London: HMSO.

Great Britain. Parliament (1987b) *Housing: The Government's Proposals*, London: HMSO.

Great Britain Parliament (1988) *Report of an Enquiry into Child Abuse in Cleveland in 1987*, Cm 417, London: HMSO.

Griffiths, B., Raynor, J., and Mohan, J. (1985) *Commercial Medicine in London*, London: Greater London Council.

Griffiths, H. (1968) *Report of the Enquiry into the Collapse of Flats at*

Ronan Point, Canning Town, London: Department of the Environment.

Griffiths, R. (1988) *Community Care: Agenda for Action. Report to the Secretary of State for Social Services*, London: HMSO.

Guardian (1984a) 'Council admits black child bias', 12 October.

Guardian (1984b) 'Bus privatisation studies show runaway costs', 3 December.

Hagerstrand, T. (1969) 'What about people in Regional Science?' *Papers and Proceedings: Regional Science Association*, 24, pp. 7–24.

Hagerstrand, T. (1969) see Jones, E. and Eyles, J. *An Introduction to Social Geography*, Oxford: Oxford University Press, pp. 134–5.

Haggett, P.(1968) *Locational Analysis in Human Geography*, London: Edward Arnold.

Halsey, A. (1972) *Educational Priority. Vol. I, Problems and Policies*, London: HMSO.

Halsey, A. (1980) 'Education can compensate', *New Society*, 24 January, pp.172–3.

Halsey, A., Heath, A., and Ridge, J. (1980) *Origins and Destinations: Family Class and Destination in Modern Britain*, Oxford: Clarendon Press.

Harbridge, E. (1981) 'Districts will not help improve collaboration', *Community Care*, 2 July, p.6.

Harrison, P. (1984) 'Housing allocation and race', *New Society*, 10 January.

Harrison, P. (1985) *Inside the Inner City: Life Under the Cutting Edge*, Harmondsworth: Penguin.

Harvey, D. (1973) *Social Justice and the City*, London: Edward Arnold.

Hayek, F. (1973) *Law, Legislation and Liberty: A New Statement of the Liberal Principles of Justice and Political Economy*, London: Routledge & Kegan Paul.

Haynes, R. (1987) *Geography of Health Services In Britain*, London: Croom Helm.

Haynes, R. and Bentham, C. (1979) 'Accessibility and use of hospitals in rural areas', *Area* 11: 186–91.

Haynes, R. and Bentham, C. (1982) 'The effects of accessibility of general practitioner attendances and inpatient admissions in Norfolk, England', *Social Science and Medicine* 16: 561–4.

Haystead, J., Howarth, V., and Strachan, A. (1980) *Preschool Education and Care,* London: Hodder & Stoughton.

Henderson, J. and Karn, V. (1984) 'Race, class and the allocation of public housing in Britain', *Urban Studies* 21: 115–28.

Henley, A. (1982) *Asian Patients in Hospital and at Home*, Oxford: Oxford University Press.

Herbert, D. (1970) 'Principle component analysis and urban social structure; a study of Cardiff and Swansea', in H. Carter, W. Davies, and C. Lewis (eds) *Studies in the Geography of Wales*, ch. 5

Herbert, D. (1976) 'Urban education problems and policies', in D. Herbert and R. Johnston (eds) *Social Areas in Cities*, New York and London: Wiley.

Her Majesty's Inspectorate (HMI) (1988) Secondary Schools: An Appraisal by Her Majesty's Inspectorate. A Report based on Inspections in England 1982–1986, London: HMSO.

Higgins, J., Deakin, N., Edwards, J., and Wicks, M. (1983) *Government and Urban Povety: Inside the Policy Making Process*, Oxford: Blackwell.

Hill, F. and Michelson, W. (1981) 'Towards a geography of urban children and youth', in D. Herbert and R. Johnston (eds) *Geography and the Urban Environment* Vol 4, Chichester: Wiley.

Hirschmann, A. (1970) *Exit, Voice and Loyalty*, Cambridge, Mass.: Harvard Univesity Press.

Home Affairs Committee (1986) *Bangladeshis in Britain. Volume I, Report with Proceedings of the Committee*, London: HMSO.

House of Commons (1981) *Racial Disadvantage. Fifth Request from the Home Affairs Committee*, London: HMSO.

Hubbock, J. and Carter, S. (1980) *Half a Chance?*, London: Commission for Racial Equality.

Hughes, J., McNaught, A., and Pennell, I. (eds) (1984) *Race and Employment in the NHS*, London: King Edward's Hospital Fund for London.

Hunt, A. (1978) *The Elderly at Home. A Study of People Aged Sixty-five and Over in England and Wales in 1976*, London: HMSO.

Hunt, S., McEwen, J., and McKenna, S. (1985) 'Social inequalities and perceived health', *Effective Health Care* 2: 151–60.

Hunt, S., Martin, C., and Platt, S. (1986) 'Housing and health in a deprived area of Edinburgh, in *Unhealthy Housing. A Diagnosis Conference of the Institute of Environmental Health Officers, Warwick University, 14–16 December 1986: Proceedings*, IEHO.

Hunt, S., McEwen, J., and McKenna, S. (1987) *Measuring Health Status*, London: Croom Helm.

Imber, V. (1977) *A Classification of Local Authorities in England and Wales*, London: HMSO.

Independent (1986) 'The cost of economic lunacy', 21 October, p.7.

Ingram, D. (1983) 'Changes in the size and age structure of London's Population 1971–1981', *Geography* 68: 56–60.

Jackson, H. (1986) 'Child accidents and housing', in *Unhealthy Housing. A Diagnosis Conference of the Institute of Environmental Health Officers, Warwick University, 14-16 December 1986: Proceedings*, IEHO.

Jackson, P. (1976) *Local Government*, London: Butterworth.

Jackson, P. (1985) 'Social geography: race and racism progress', *Human Geography* 9(1): 99–108

Jackson, P., and Smith, S. (eds) (1981) *Social Integration and Ethnic Segregation*, New York and London: Academic Press.

Jarman, B. (1983) 'Identification of under-privileged areas', *British Medical Journal* 286: 1705–8.

Jenkins, J. and Rose, H. (1976) 'Rate support grants and their application to London', *Greater London Intelligence Quarterly* 35, pp. 9–26

Jervis, M. (1986) 'Different but not unhealthy', *Health Service Journal*, 21 August, p. 1105.

Johnson, M. (1986) 'Inner city residents, ethnic minorities and primary health care in the West Midlands', in T. Rathwell and D. Phillips (eds) *Health, Race and Ethnicity*, London: Croom Helm, pp. 192–212.

Joint Tuberculosis Committee (1978) 'Tuberculosis among immigrants in the UK: the role of occupational health services', *British Medical Journal*, 22 April, p. 1038.

Jones, E. and Eyles, J. (1977) *Introduction to Social Geography*, Oxford: Oxford University Press.

Jones, G. and Stewart, J. (1985) *The Case for Local Government* (2nd ed), London: Allen & Unwin.

Jones, K. and Moon, G. (1987) *Health Disease and Society*, London: Routledge & Kegan Paul.

Jones, L., Leneman, L., and Maclean, U. (1987) *Consumer Feedback for the NHS: A Literature Review*, London: King Edward's Hospital Fund for London.

Jones, P. (1979) 'Ethnic areas in British cities', in D. Herbert and D. Smith (eds) *Social Problems and the City*, Oxford: Oxford University Press.

Joseph, A. and Phillips, D. (1984) *Accessibility and Utilisation: Geographical Perspectives on Health Delivery*, New York: Harper & Row.

Judge, K., Ferlie, E., Smith, T. (1982) *Home Help Charges*, London: Policy Studies Institute.

Karn, V. (1977) *Retiring to the Seaside*, London: Routledge & Kegan Paul.

Keith-Lucas, B. and Richards, P. (1976) *A History of Local Government in the Twentieth Century*, London: Allen & Unwin.

Kelmer Pringle, M. (1975) *The Needs of Children*, London: Hutchinson.

Kemp, P. (1984) *The Cost of Chaos. A Survey of the Housing Benefit Scheme*, SHAC Research Report No. 8, London: SHAC.

Kemp, P. and Raynsford, N. (1984) *Housing Benefit: The Evidence. A Collection of Submissions to the Housing Benefit Review*, London: Housing Centre Trust.

Kempe, R. and Kempe, C. (1976) *Child Abuse: The Developing Child*, London: Fontana.

Khogali, M. (1979) 'Tuberculosis among immigrants in the UK: the role of occupational health services', *Journal of Epidemiology and Community Health* 33: 134–7.

Knapp, M. (1984) *The Economics of Social Care*, London: Macmillan.

Lambert, L. and Rowe, J. (1973) *Children Who Wait*, London: Association of British Adoption Agencies.

Lauglo, M. (1984) *The Spitalfields Survey*, Tower Hamlets Department of Community Health, London.

Law, C. and Warnes, A. (1982) 'The destination decision in retirement migration', in A. Warnes (ed.) *Geographical Perspectives on the Elderly*, London: Wiley, pp. 53–82.

Leach, P. (1979) *Who Cares? A New Deal for Mothers and their Small Children*, Harmondsworth: Penguin.

153

References

Le Grand, J. (1982) *The Strategy of Equality: Redistribution and the Social Services*, London: Allen & Unwin.

Le Grand, J. and Illsley, R. (1987) 'The measurement of inequality in health', in A. Williams (ed.) *Health and Economics*, London: Macmillan, pp. 12–36.

Levitt, R. (1984) *The Reorganised National Health Services* (3rd edn), London: Croom Helm.

Lewis, R. (1952) *Edwin Chadwick and the Public Health Movement, 1832–1854*, London: Longman.

Little, A. (1985) 'Education for whom?', *New Society*, 21 March, pp. 449–50.

Little, A. and Mabey, C. (1973) 'Reading attainment and ethnic mix of London's primary schools', in D. Donnbon (ed.) *London: Urban Patterns and Problems and Policies*.

Littlewood, J. and Tinker, A. (1981) *Families in Flats*, Department of the Environment, London: HMSO.

London Health Planning Consortium (1981) *Primary Health Care in Inner London*, London: DHSS.

Lumb, K., Congdon, P., and Lealman, G. (1981) 'A comparative review of Asian and British born maternity patients in Bradford 1974–8', *Journal of Epidemiology and Community Health* 35: 106–9.

MacFarlane, A. and Fox, A. (1978) 'Child deaths from accident and violence', *Population Trends* 12.

McIntosh, N. and Smith, D. (1974) *The Extent of Racial Discrimination, PEP Report 547*, Political and Economic Planning, London: Policy Studies Institute.

McNaught, A. (1983) *Race and Health Care in the United Kingdom. Occasional Papers in Health Services Administration*, London: Centre for Health Service Management Studies/Polytechnic of the South Bank.

Mair, R. (1979) 'Health services', in J. English and F. Martin (eds) *Social Services in Scotland*, Edinburgh: Scottish Academic Press, pp. 55–75.

Maltby, D. and White, H. (1982) *The Geography of Transport in England and Wales*, London: Methuen.

Marmot, M., Adestein, A., and Bulusu, L. (1983) 'Immigrant mortality in England', *Population Trends* 33: 14–17.

Marsh, C. (1986) *The Survey Method: The Contribution of Surveys to Social Explanation*, Contemporary Social Research No. 6, London: Allen & Unwin.

Marshall, G., Newby, H., Rose, D., and Vogler, C. (1988) *Social Class in Modern Britain*, London: Hutchinson.

Maslow, A. (1954) *Motivation and Personality*, New York: Harper & Row.

Massam, B. (1975) *Location and Space in Social Administration*, London: Edward Arnold.

Matthews, M. (1981) 'Children's perception of urban distance', *Area* 13(4): 333–44

Matthews, M. (1984) 'Environmental cognition of young children: images of the journey to school and home area', *Transactions of Institute of British Geographers* 9(1): 89–100.

Mayhew, L. and Leonardi, G. (1982) 'Equity, efficiency and accessibility in urban and regional health care systems', *Environment and Planning A* 14:1479–1507.

Mayhew, L. (1986) *Urban Hospital Location*, London: Allen & Unwin.

Midwinter, A., and Mair, C. (1987) *Rates Reform*, Edinburgh: Mainstream Publishing.

Mohan, J. (1985) 'Independent acute medical care in Britain: its organisation, location and future prospects', *International Journal of Urban and Regional Research* 9(4): 467–84.

Mohan, J. and Woods, K. (1985) 'Restructuring health care: the social geography of public and private health care under the British Conservative government', *International Journal of Health Services* 15(2): 197–215.

Moseley, M. (1979) *Accessibility: The Rural Challenge*, London: Methuen.

Moseley, M., and Spencer, M. (1978) 'Access to shops: the situation in rural Norfolk', p. 33–44, in M. Moseley (ed) (1978) *Social Issues in Rural Norfolk*, Norwich: Centre for East Anglia Studies, University of East Anglia.

Moss, P. (1978) *Alternative Models of Group Child Care for Preschool Children with Working Parents*, London: Equal Opportunties Commission.

Moyland, S., Millar, J., and Davies, R. (1984) *For Richer for Poorer. DHSS Cohort Study of Unemployed Men. DHSS Social Research Branch*, Research Report No. 11, London: HMSO.

Murdie, R. (1969) *Factorial Ecology of Metropolitan Toronto 1951–61*, Research Paper 116, Chicago: Chicago University Geography Department.

Murray, N. (1985) 'Turning the tide', *Community Care*, 21 November, pp. 23–5.

Musgrave, R. (1969) *Fiscal Systems*, New Haven, Conn.: Yale University Press.

Musgrave, R. and Musgrave, P. (1980) *Public Finance in Theory and Practice*, New York: McGraw-Hill.

Navarro, V. (1976) *Medicine under Capitalism*, London: Martin Robertson.

Navarro, V. (1980) 'The nature of democracy in the core capitalist countries: meanings and implications for class struggle', *Insurgent Sociologist* 10: 3–15.

New Society (1984a), 'Educational achievement', 15 March, pp. i–iv.

New Society (1984b) 'Report: what the councils spent', 26 April, p. 159.

New Society (1984c) 'Black, brown and white', 6 December, p. 359.

Newton, K. and Karran, T. (1985) *The Politics of Local Expenditure*, London: Macmillan.

Observer (1984) 'The lessons from Ronan Point', 13 October.

Office of Population Censuses and Surveys (OPCS)(1980a) *Registrar-General's Classification of Occupations*, London: HMSO.

OPCS (1980b) *General Household Survey, 1979*, London: HMSO.

OPCS (1981) *General Household Survey, 1979*, London: HMSO.

OPCS (1982) *Sources of Statistics on Ethnic Minorities*, OPCS Monitor

PP1 82/1, London: OPCS.

OPCS (1983a) *General Household Survey, 1982*, London: HMSO.

OPCS (1983b) *A Census Atlas*, London: HMSO.

OPCS (1984a) *Census Guide 1, Britain's Elderly Population: Census 1981*, London: OPCS.

OPCS (1984b) *Census Guide 2, Children and Families: Census 1981*, London: OPCS.

OPCS (1985a) *Mid-1984 Population Estimates for Local Government Areas and Health Authority Areas of England and Wales*, OPCS Monitor PP1 85/2, London: OPCS.

OPCS (1985b) *Live Births during 1984*, OPCS Monitor FM1/85/1, London: OPCS.

OPCS (1985c) *General Household Survey Preliminary Results for 1984*, OPCS Monitor GHS 1985/1, London: OPCS.

OPCS (1986a) *General Household Survey, 1984*, London: HMSO.

OPCS (1986b) *Labour Force Survey, 1985: Ethnic Group and Country of Birth*, OPCS Monitor L 86/2, London: OPCS. @REFERENCE = OPCS (1986c) *Key Population and Vital Statistics. Local and Health Authority Areas Series VS*, London: HMSO.

OPCS (1987) *Family Expenditure Survey, 1987*, London: HMSO.

Osborne, A., Butler, N., and Morris, A. (1984) *The Social Life of Britain's Five Year Olds: A Report of the Child Health and Education Study*, London: Routledge & Kegan Paul.

Owen, S. (1978) 'Changing accessibility in two Norfolk villages', in M. Moseley (ed) *Social Issues in Rural Norfolk*, Norwich: University of East Anglia, pp. 13–32.

Packman, J. (1975) *The Child's Generation. Child Care Policy from Curtis to Houghton*, Oxford: Blackwell.

Pahl, J. (1980) 'Patterns of money management in marriage', *Journal of Social Policy* 9(3): 313–15.

Pahl, J. (1985) 'Who benefits from child benefit?' *New Society*, 25 April, pp. 117–19.

Palmer, D. and Gleave, D. (1981) 'Employment, housing and mobility in London', *London Journal* 7(2): 177–93.

Parker, R. (1980) *Caring for Separated Children,* London: Macmillan.

Parsons, T. and Shills, E. (eds) (1951) *Towards a General Theory of Action,* Cambridge, Mass.: Harvard University Press.

Peace, S. (1982) 'The activity pattern of elderly people in Swansea, South Wales, and south-east England', in A. Warnes (ed.) *Geographical Perspectives on the Elderly*, London: Wiley, pp. 281–301.

Peace, S. (1986) 'Residential accommodation for dependent elderly people in Britain: the relationship between spatial structure and individual lifestyle', Espace Populations Societés, 1987: 281–90.

Peach, C. (1982) 'The growth and distribution of the black population in Britain, 1945–1980', in D. Coleman (ed.) *Demography of Immigrants and Minority Groups in the United Kingdom,* London: Academic Press.

Peach, C. (1984) 'The force of West Indian island identity in Britain', in C. Clarke, D. Ley, and C. Peach (eds) *Geography and Ethnic*

Pluralism, London: Allen & Unwin. pp. 214–30.

Phillips, D. (1979) 'Spatial variations in attendance at general practitioner services', *Social Science and Medicine* 13D: 169–81.

Phillips, D. and Vincent, J. (1986) 'Private Residential Accommodation for the Elderly: Geographical Aspects of Developments in Devon', *Transactions of the Institute of British Geographers* (n.s.), II: 150–73

Phillips, D. and Williams, A. (1984) *Rural Britain: A Social Geography*, Oxford: Blackwell.

Piaget, J. (1969) *The Psychology of the Child*, London: Routledge & Kegan Paul.

Piche, D. (1981) 'The spontaneous geography of the urban child', in D. Herbert and R. Johnston (eds) *Geography and the Urban Environment*, London: Wiley, Vol. 4, pp. 229–56.

Pinch, S. (1980) 'Local authority provision for the elderly: an overview and case study of London', in D. Herbert and R. Johnston (eds) *Geography and the Urban Environment*, London: Wiley, Vol. 3, pp. 295–343.

Pinch, S. (1985) *Cities and Services*, London: Routledge & Kegan Paul.

Pinch, S. (1987) 'Labour market theory: quantification and policy', *Environment and Planning A* 19: 1477–94.

Power, A. (1988) *Council Housing: Conflict, Change and Decision Making*, Welfare State Programme Discussion Paper No. 27, London: Suntory Toyota International Centre for Economics and Related Disciplines/ London School of Economics.

Ranson, S., Jones, G., and Walsh, K. (eds) (1985) *Between Centre and Locality: The Politics of Public Policy*, London: Allen & Unwin.

Rathwell, T. and Phillips, D. (eds) (1986) *Health, Race and Ethnicity*, London: Croom Helm.

Rawls, J. (1972) *A Theory of Justice*, Cambridge, Mass.: Harvard University Press.

Redcliffe-Maude, Lord, and Wood, B. (1974) *English Local Government Reformed*, London: Oxford University Press.

Rex, J. (1971) 'The concept of housing class and the sociology of race relations', *Race* 12(3): 282–301.

Rex, J. and Moore, R. (1967) *Race, Community and Conflict*, Oxford: Oxford University Press.

Ritchie, J., Jacoby, A., and Bone, M. (1981) *Access to Primary Care*, London: HMSO.

Rivett, G. (1986) *Development of the London Hospital System 1823-1982*, London: King's Fund.

Robinson, P. (1976) *Education and Poverty*, London: Methuen.

Robinson, V. (1984) 'Asians in Britain: a study of encapsulation and marginality', in C. Clarke, D. Ley, and C. Peach (eds) *Geography and Ethnic Pluralism*, London: Allen & Unwin.

Robson, B. (1969) *Urban Analysis: A Study of City Structure*, Cambridge: Cambridge University Press.

Robson, B. (1979) 'Housing empiricism and the state', in D. Herbert and D. Smith (eds) *Social Problems and the City*, Oxford: Oxford University Press.

References

Rowles, G. (1980) *Prisoners of Space? Exploring the Geographical Experience of Older People*, USA, Westpoint Press.

Rowntree, B. (1902) *Poverty: A Study of Town Life*, London: Longman.

Runnymede Trust and the Radical Stastistics Race Group (1980) *Britain's Black Population*, London: Heinemann Educational Books.

Rushton, G. (1969) 'Analysis of spatial behaviour by revealed space preferences', *Annals of the Association of American Geographers* 55: 391–400.

Samuelson, P. (1954) 'Pure theory of public expenditures', *Review of Economics and Statistics* 36: 386–9.

Selden, A. (ed) (1980) *Town Hall Power or Whitehall Pawn?* London: Institute of Economic Affairs.

Sheiham, M. and Quick, A. (1982) *The Rickets Report*, London: Haringey Community Health Council.

Shevky, E. and Bell, W. (1955) *Social Area Analysis: Theory, Illustrative Application and Computational Procedure*, Stanford, Calif.

Shevky, E. and Williams, M. (1949) *The Social Areas of Los Angeles: Analysis and Typology*, Berkeley, Calif.

Sillitoe, K. (1987) 'Questions on race and ethnicity and related topics for the Census', *Population Trends* 49: 5–11.

Silman, A., Laysen, E., De Graaf, W., and Sramak, M. (1985) 'High dietary fat intake and cigarette smoking as risk factors for ischeamic heart disease in Bangladeshi male immigrants in East London', *Journal of Epidemiology and Community Health* 39(4): 301–3.

Simey, T.S. and Simey, M.B. (1960) *Charles Booth: Social Scientist*, Oxford: Oxford University Press.

Simpson, A. (1984) *Stacking the Decks: A Study of Race Inequality and Council Housing in Nottingham*, Nottingham: NDCRC.

Skelton, N. (1977) *Travel Patterns of Elderly People under a Concessionary Fares Scheme*, Supplementary Report 280, Transport and Road Research Laboratory, Crowthorne.

Skelton, N. (1982) 'Transport policies and the elderly', in A. Warnes (ed.) *Geographical Perspectives on the Elderly*, London: Wiley, pp. 303–22.

Sloan, F. and Bentkover, J. (1979) *Access to Ambulatory Care and the U.S. Economy*, Lexington MA: Lexington Books.

Smellie, K. (1968) *A History of Local Government*, London: Allen & Unwin.

Smith, D. (1977) *Human Geography: A Welfare Approach*, London: Edward Arnold.

Smith, D. (1979) *Where the Grass is Greener: Geographical Perspectives on Inequality*, London: Croom Helm.

Smith, J. and Grant, R. (1982) 'The elderly's travel in the Costwolds', in A. Warnes (ed.) *Geographical Perspectives on the Elderly*, London: Wiley, pp. 323.

Smith, M. (1980) *The City and Social Theory*, New York: St Martin's Press.

Spencer, C. and Dixon, J. (1983) 'Mapping the development of feelings about the city', *Transactions of the Institute of British Geographers* 3: 373.

Stoker, G. (1988) *The Politics of Local Government*, London: Macmillan.

Stone, M. (1981) *The Education of Black Children*, London: Fontana.

The Times (1984) 'Special report: the metropolitan counties', 14 December, pp. 15–18.

Thisse, J.-F. and Zoller, H. (eds) (1983) *Locational Analysis of Public Facilities*, Oxford: North Holland.

Thomas, D. (1984a) 'The jobs bias against blacks', *New Society*, 1 November, pp. 167–9.

Thomas, D. (1984b) 'A fairer deal for blacks on jobs', *New Society*, 8 November, pp. 208–10.

Thunhurst, C. (1985) 'The analysis of small area statistics and planning for health', *Statistician* 34: 93–106.

Tiebout, C. (1956) 'A pure theory of local expenditure', *Journal of Political Economy* 64: 416–24.

Townsend, P. (1979) *Poverty in the United Kingdom*, Harmondsworth: Penguin.

Townsend, P. and Davidson, N. (1982) *Inequalities in Health*, Harmondsworth: Penguin.

Townsend, P., Davidson, N., and Whitehead, M. (1988) *Inequalities in Health and the Health Divide*, Harmondsworth: Penguin.

Townsend, P., Phillimore, P., and Beattie, A. (1988) *Health Deprivation and Inequality and the North*, London: Croom Helm.

Tudor-Hart, J. (1971) 'The inverse care law', *Lancet* i: 405.

Tunstall, P., Clayton, D., Morris, J., Brigate, W., and McDonald, L., (1975) 'Coronary attacks in East London', *Lancet* ii: 833–8.

Twine, F. and Williams, N. (1983) 'Social segregation in public sector housing: a case study', *Transactions of Institution of British Geographers* (n.s.), 8(3): 253–66.

Walters, V. (1981) *Class Inequality and Health Care*, London: Croom Helm.

Warnes, A. and Law, C. (1982) 'The destination decision in retirement migration', in A. Warnes (ed.) *Geographical Perspectives on the Elderly*, London: Wiley, pp. 53–82.

Warnes, A. and Law, C. (1984) 'The elderly population of Great Britain; locational trends and policy implications', *Transactions Institute of British Geographers* (n.s.), 9: 37–59.

Weber, M. (1958) *The City*, Chicago: The Free Press.

Webber, R. (1975) *Liverpool Social Area Study 1971 Data: Final Report*, Liverpool: Planning Research Applications Group.

Webber, R. (1977a) *Social Area Analysis of Greater London*, Liverpool: Planning Research Applications Group.

Webber, R. (1977b) *Cumbria Social Area Analysis*, Liverpool: Planning Research Applications Group.

Webber, R. (1977c) 'The national classification of residential neighbourhoods', in *Introduction to the Classfication of Wards and Parishes*, Liverpool: Planning Research Applications Group.

Webber, R. and Craig, J. (1978) *Socio-Economic Classifications of Local Authority Areas*, OPCS Studies in Medical and Population Subjects No. 35, London: HMSO.

References

Wedge, J. and Prosser, M. (1973) *Born to Fail*, London: Arrow.

White, J.(1980) *The Worst Street in North London*, London: Routledge & Kegan Paul.

Whitehead, M. (1987) *The Health Divide: Health Inequalities in the 1980s*, London: Health Education Authority.

Williams, P. (1978) 'Urban managerialism: a concept of relevance?' *Area* 10: 236–40.

Williams, R. (1976) 'The role of institutions in the inner London housing market', *Transactions of the Institute of British Geographers* (n.s.), 1: 72–81.

Williamson, W. and Bryne, D. (1979) 'Educational disadvantage in an urban setting', in D. Herbert and D. Smith (eds) *Social Problems in the City*, Oxford: Oxford University Press, ch. 10.

Wilson, A. (1974) *Urban and Regional Models in Geography and Planning*, London: Wiley.

Wirth, L. (1938) 'Urbanism as a way of life', *American Journal of Sociology* 44: 1–24.

Wistow, G. and Fuller, S. (1986) *Joint Planning in Perspective*, Birmingham: National Association of Health Authorities/Centre for Research in Social Policy, Loughborough University.

Young, M. and Willmott, P. (1957) *Family and Kinship in East London*, Harmondsworth: Penguin.

Young, K. and Connelly, N. (1981) *Policy and Practice in the Multi-Racial City*, London: Policy Studies Institute.

Index

Able, R. (*et al.*) 6
Aday. L. (*et al.*) 138
access/accessibility 3, 90, 92, 138
Acts (of Parliament): Housing
    Act, 1946 54; Housing Act,
    1980 58; Housing Act, 1988
    53; Housing (Homeless
    Persons) Act, 1977 54;
    Housing and Town Planning
    Act, 1919 54; Housing
    Benefits Act, 1982 61;
    Housing Subsidies Act, 1956
    55; Education Act, 1870 49;
    Education Act, 1902 49;
    Education Act, 1918 49;
    Education Act, 1944 49–51;
    Education Act, 1976 52;
    Education Act, 1980 50, 52;
    Education Reform Act, 1988
    50, 52, 139; Local Authority
    Social Services Act, 1970 39;
    Local Government Act, 1871
    26, 27; Local Government
    Act, 1929 28, 29; Local
    Government Act, 1888 26;
    Local Government Act, 1894
    26; Local Government Act,
    1972 29, 30; Local
    Government Act, 1985 29,
    34; Local Government Grants
    (Social Need) Act, 1969 75;
    Local Government, Planning
    and Land Act 58; Local
    Government, Scotland, Act,
    1929 34; Local Government,
    Scotland, Act, 1973 35;
    London Government Act,
    1963 29; Municipal
Corporations Act, 1835 25,
    26; National Assistance Act,
    1948 93; National Health
    Service Act, 1946 125;
    Public Health Act 1848 26,
    27; Public Health Act 1875
    26; Race Relations Act, 1975
    103; Rating and Valuation
    Act, 1925 122; Transport
    Act, 1968 62;
administration of local
    government 22–37
Advisory Council on Child Care
    72
Ahmed, S. 102
Aiach, P. (*et al.*) 15
Anderson, T. (and Egland, J.)
    128
Arnold, E. 114
Association of County Councils
    41
Association of Metropolitan
    Authorities 54, 61
Atkinson, A. (*et al.*) 10, 70
Audit commission 44, 58, 139
Avon county 32, 33

Babbage, A. 57
Bagley, C. (*et al.*) 108
Balchin, P. 53, 54, 57, 58, 93
Bandaranayke, R. 111, 113
Barnard, K. 92
Barnes J. (and Lucas H.) 76
Bebbington A. (*et al.*) 78, 96,
    128, 129
Bell, C. (and Newby, H.) 142
Bangladeshis 104, 110
Bennett, R. 1, 2, 117, 121, 141